I0119450

University Johns Hopkins

John Hopkins University Studies in Historical and Political Science

Science

Extra Volume XVIII

University Johns Hopkins

John Hopkins University Studies in Historical and Political Science
Extra Volume XVIII

ISBN/EAN: 9783744777896

Printed in Europe, USA, Canada, Australia, Japan

Cover: Foto ©Suzi / pixelio.de

More available books at **www.hansebooks.com**

JOHNS HOPKINS UNIVERSITY STUDIES

IN

HISTORICAL AND POLITICAL SCIENCE

HERBERT B. ADAMS, Editor

History is past Politics and Politics are present History.—*Freeman*

EXTRA VOLUME

XVIII

PRINTED BY

The Friedenwald Company

BALTIMORE, MD., U.S.A.

CONTENTS.

STATE AID TO HIGHER EDUCATION

AN ADDRESS

BY

HON. CHARLES K. ADAMS, LL. D.

President of the University of Wisconsin and lately President of Cornell University

DELIVERED AT THE TWENTY-SECOND ANNIVERSARY OF THE
JOHNS HOPKINS UNIVERSITY, FEBRUARY 22, 1898

It has sometimes been asserted, and at other times been assumed, that the policy of supporting higher education by the State is in this country practically a new policy, or one which does not rest upon a traditional or historical foundation. While everyone at all familiar with the trend of educational affairs must admit that the growth of State universities is one of the most remarkable features of recent educational development, very few seem to be aware of the fact that State assistance to education, in all its branches, has been the traditional policy of the country. Not long since I heard an eloquent address on State universities, in which the speaker admitted that the movement was irresistible. He declared that it could no more be stopped, either by denominational prejudice, or by outcries against socialism or by the advocates of *laissez faire*, than the building of railroads and the running of trains across the plains can be stopped by the shouts of Indians or the showers of Indian arrows. Occasionally, he said, an engineer or a fireman may be shot down, but his place is at once filled and the work goes on as before. So it was, he said, with the inevitable progress of the State universities. But in

all his discourse there was an assumption that the movement is essentially a new one; one that does not rest on any
historical basis, but is simply one of the many beneficent
innovations of this age of progress.

Such an assumption may be easily accounted for. It is
true that seventy-five, or fifty, or even twenty-five years
ago, the policy of supporting universities by the State did
not attract the very general attention of the public. The
older institutions, which, during their infancy, had been
nursed into vigor and efficiency by public support, had
been turned over to the care of their wealthy children, and
had ceased to be dependent upon their parents. Schools
of learning, established either by denominational zeal or
by private benevolence, had sprung up in all parts of the
country. These two facts had completely shut out of view
the true historical sequence of educational development.

But notwithstanding these more or less general impressions, it is nevertheless true that beneath and back of these
specious appearances is the great fact that during the whole
of the first two hundred years of our history, education in
all of its grades was chiefly supported by the taxation of all
the people. This is neither the time nor the place to
multiply or to dwell upon details; the briefest possible
notice of our educational methods in Colonial times will
be enough in this connection to show our general traditional
policy.

The great university at Cambridge is sometimes said to
have been founded by John Harvard; but such a statement
is true only in a very limited sense, for before that benefactor contributed the half of his fortune and the whole of
his library and his name to the college an appropriation for
that purpose had been made by the general court of the
colony. This was only six years after the founding of
Boston and six years before the establishment of the famous
school system of Massachusetts Bay.

One of the Massachusetts antiquarians has pointed out
that the Colonial Legislature, before the end of the eigh-

teenth century, made more than one hundred different appropriations for the college, an average of as many as one every two years. When the Revolution came on and the State was called upon to adopt a new constitution, it was but the natural continuation of the same beneficent policy that led the constitution to command all future Legislatures, in the most elaborate and specific terms, to care for all the interests of education, and especially the University at Cambridge. It is an extraordinary fact that the whole of Chapter V. of the Constitution of 1780 is entitled: "The University at Cambridge and Encouragement of Literature." No one can read that remarkable chapter without being impressed with the idea that the people of Massachusetts considered Harvard College at that moment as an institution that in all future time must have the most tender and the most thoughtful care of all the people of the State.[1] In the same generation, and in the same spirit, Nathan Dane secured for the endowment and support of secondary schools a very generous appropriation of lands in that part of Massachusetts which now constitutes the State of Maine. Whether it was this same Nathan Dane, as Daniel Webster asserted, or Dr. Manasseh Cutler, as Dr. Poole afterward contended, that secured the most important provisions of the "Ordinance of 1787" for the organization of the Northwest, it is certain that it was this very spirit of the Massachusetts Constitution that was embodied in that famous ordinance. You remember that besides providing for free navigation of the rivers, the establishment of the English common law and the prohibition of slavery forever, it asserted that "schools and the means of education shall forever be encouraged."

The course of Massachusetts is not unique nor even peculiar. When, in 1701, Yale was founded, the Legislature gave a helping hand, and in the course of the century so generous and so numerous were the legislative gifts for

---

[1] Further illustration of the statement of President Adams will be found on page 22.

endowment, for current expenses and for buildings, that the first President Dwight, at the end of the last century, declared that the State of Connecticut had been the chief benefactor of Yale College.[1]

It might be pointed out that a similar spirit prevailed in the establishment and support of the older colleges in the southern part of the country.

I trust you will pardon me for recalling to your recollection the fact that in the State of Maryland, as early as 1692, the Legislature passed an act for the encouragement of learning, and that in 1723 provision was made for the establishment of a school of a higher grade in every county in the province. Aid was given in money, lands were appropriated and a poll-tax of twenty shillings was required to be paid on negroes and other servants. What followed? In 1782 the school in Kent county had met with such success that it applied for legislative aid, with the result that it received from the Legislature a charter as " Washington College." Two years later the King William School, at Annapolis, was converted by the same authority and for the same reasons into " St. John's College." These together were denominated the " University of Maryland."

In North Carolina, Chapter XLI. of the Constitution of 1776 provided that " all useful learning shall be duly encouraged and promoted in one or more universities."

In South Carolina the legislative act of 1700 for the general establishment of schools was followed in 1785 by the establishment of three colleges in one day, and within twenty-five years more than three-fourths of a million dollars were appropriated by the Legislature for the support of these institutions.

In Virginia, William and Mary was from the first the ward of the colony, and it was even while the Revolutionary War was raging that Jefferson urged upon the House of Burgesses his remarkable scheme for a comprehensive

[1] See p. 23.

system of education that should be supported by general taxation and should culminate in a university and in the liberal establishment of secondary schools.

One word more needs to be said in regard to the educational characteristics of the Colonial period.

In the North there seems to have been an adequate appreciation of the fact that the higher education, to be successful, must be concentrated within comparatively few institutions. This is shown by several incidents in the history of the founding of Yale College, for, in the course of the seventeenth century, the founding of a college in Connecticut was several times considered by the Colonial Legislature. Again and again bills were introduced, but until the beginning of the next century it was repeatedly decided that the population of New England was not yet sufficient to support more than one college and, therefore, that their energies should not be devoted to the establishment of a second institution. And it was for this reason and for this only that the establishment of Yale College did not take place until more than 60 years after the founding of Harvard.

The speaker then referred to other Eastern institutions and said:

Now, if we turn from the East to the West, or rather from the thirteen original States to the new territory beyond the Alleghenies, we find that somewhat analogous conditions have prevailed. We see that successes and failures have resulted from essentially the same causes.

Look for a moment at the development of State education. The injunction of the "Ordinance of 1787" was promptly acted upon. The very first session of the First Congress provided for the organization of the Northwest Territorial government and appropriated lands for the establishment of a university in Ohio; and from that day to this it has been the policy of Congress, to which there has not been a single exception, to give at least two townships of land in every State for the support of a university.

Before 1821 it was estimated that more than 6,000,000
acres of land had been appropriated by Congress to the
purposes of higher education. These gifts, as you all
know, and I trust that you will pardon me for recounting
facts that are so well known, have been supplemented by
the liberal Morrill act in 1862, by the Hatch act in 1889,
and by the supplementary Morrill act in 1890. Thus, no
State has been admitted to the Union since the adoption
of the Constitution that has not received from the general
government the means for the establishment and support
of higher education in substantial accordance with the
policy which existed throughout the Colonial period.[1]

But there is another analogy between the two periods
that is of supreme interest. In some of the Western States
the policy prevails which was characteristic of the North;
in others the policy prevailed which was characteristic of
the South. For example, in Ohio, in Indiana, and in
Illinois, the funds arising from the sale of these lands, in-
stead of being concentrated in the development of one
institution, were divided and given to two or more. On the
other hand, in Michigan, in Wisconsin, and in Minnesota,
the funds were concentrated and were given in each of the
States to a single university. The results have been entirely analogous to those which prevailed in the East during
the Colonial period. In Ohio, Indiana and Illinois the
State institutions during their early years were comparatively feeble and unimportant, while in the northern tier of
States the policy of concentration, whatever its vicissitudes,
from time to time has been crowned with remarkable
success.

But while such have been the general results, perhaps I
should guard against leaving the impression that either success or failure has been without its vicissitudes. Even
where the policy of concentration has been followed, there
have been differences of methods that have caused a variety

[1] See p. 17.

of results. For example, the State of Michigan was exceptionally fortunate in the ability and the learning of the men to whom the interests of higher education were at first intrusted. Not only was the organization of the educational system unusually wise, but the administration of the lands was conducted with such exceptional skill that the university was generously supported from this source during all the early years of its history. It was not until thirty years after the founding of the university at Ann Arbor that the first appropriation to the university was made by the State. Fortunately, it may be said that from 1867 to the present day every Legislature, with a single exception, has shown its interest in the university by liberal appropriations.[1]

In Wisconsin, on the other hand, a different policy was pursued. The State came into the Union at the moment when streams of immigration were pouring over the Alleghenies into the West from all parts of the world. It was avowedly for the purpose of attracting immigration that the university lands, and for the most part also, even the common school lands, were thrown upon the market at nominal prices. The policy was adopted of intrusting to the future Legislatures of the State the responsibility of supporting the schools of all grades which the people in the future were to enjoy. The consequence was that during its early years the University of Wisconsin was comparatively feeble, and it was not until the State aroused itself to redeem the pledge it had given when it sacrificed the university lands, that the university came forward to take its place among the most prosperous in the country.[1]

Nor should it be supposed that the history of State institutions has been free from perplexities and trying vicissitudes. Juvenile diseases are not the peculiarities of individuals alone. But just as these diseases, however annoying and perplexing, are no reason for abandoning humanity as a failure, so it may be said that in the history of education experience has shown that the vitality and strength of the

[1] See p. 19.

system as a whole have generally been sufficient to overcome all the weaknesses and the corruptions of early years, and bring the universities out into the triumphant strength and prosperity of vigorous manhood. Ignorance in regard to methods of organization, the spirit of peculation and speculation, too often characteristic of frontier civilization, even the cupidity of grasping and dishonest men and the insane desire for crude and absurd innovations, have, as a rule, sooner or later given way to a just respect for the results of experience and an inflexible determination to provide liberally from the common treasury for the common good. Even those States which have been most unfortunate in their early history have finally come to see their mistakes, and have done everything possible to correct them. In the end the States have almost, or quite, without exception, profited by their early follies, and have settled down to wiser methods.

Ohio has given up the effort to nurse its three State colleges into greatness and has concentrated its liberality upon the new State University at Columbus. Indiana, reluctant to give up widely separated buildings and equipment, and unwilling to incur the criticism of interested localities, still persists in dividing its support between two institutions. Illinois has at length come to see the path of manifest destiny, and is giving liberal support to the long neglected University at Champaign. The other State universities have generally been framed with greater or less fidelity upon the successful model of Michigan, and they are all now supported chiefly by legislative appropriations.

The same spirit has prevailed with regard to schools of secondary grade. Everywhere the high school is the centre of local educational interest. Attention has often been called to the fact that the high school throughout the eastern part of the country is so overshadowing the private schools that only those academies that are richly endowed find it easy to resist the tendency to decay. A still more irresistible tendency in the same direction is dominant in the newer States, for the reason that in those regions the private academies never get a fair start. The consequence is that the high school is everywhere. Its building is often the most conspicuous structure in the frontier town and the chief object of civic pride. Chicago has twelve high schools, each with its four-year courses, organized to furnish a good fitting for college. Michigan has more schools of this grade than has Massachusetts, and Wisconsin and Iowa have more in proportion to their population than has Connecticut. Not only is the number of schools greater, but the number of pupils in the schools is greater. According to the report of the Commissioner of Education for 1895-6, recently published, the total number of pupils in secondary schools in the North Atlantic Division in 1895-6 was 168,529, while the number in the North Central Division was 248,962. In point of numbers there were 80,000 more in the North Central Division than in the North Atlantic Division.

Nor is this striking difference accounted for by an excess of population, for the same authority shows that in every 1000 inhabitants there are in the secondary schools of all classes in the North Atlantic Division 8.06 pupils; while in every 1000 inhabitants in the North Central Division there are as many as 10.03 pupils. In other words, in the North Central Division, in every 1000 of the inhabitants, the number of pupils in the schools of secondary grade, including the high schools and the academies, is about 24 per cent. greater than the number in each 1000 inhabitants of the North Atlantic States.

If this system of public support has such success in the secondary schools, what is to be said of its success in the schools of collegiate and university grade?

Unfortunately for the purposes of comparison, the State institutions of higher grade do not occupy the field alone. The condition of higher education in the Central West is analogous to the condition of secondary education in the East, in the fact that the field is occupied by both classes—

that is to say, by those institutions privately endowed and those supported by taxation. But the results of the system are not difficult to discover. The Commissioner's report already quoted gives the number of students in higher education in 1896 in the North Atlantic Division as 44,570, while in the North Central Division it was 50,290.

If we turn from these interesting figures to a study of the comparative growth of public and private institutions of higher grade, we find still more striking results. These results were presented not long since by Chancellor Mac-Lean of the University of Nebraska in his inaugural address. Though I have not verified these figures, I assume them to be correct. According to this authority, in the ten years included between 1885 and 1895 the increase of students of collegiate and university grade in the ten representative colleges and universities of New England, including Harvard and Yale, was 20 per cent.; the increase in ten representative private or denominational colleges in the North Central States was 14¼ per cent., while the increase in the ten representative State universities was no less than 320 per cent. I almost shrink from giving these figures, for I know that I am in an atmosphere where numbers count for very little and quality counts for very much; but I am sure that no one at all qualified to judge will claim that these additions have been made by any lowering of the standards. On the contrary, it is as certain that the standards are constantly rising, as it is that the numbers of students are constantly increasing. Many who have had abundant opportunities of judging will assert that the standards of scholarship in the State universities compare favorably with those of the private institutions, either in the West or in the East.

Another fact ought not to be overlooked. The tendency is everywhere growing to co-ordinate more and more closely the several grades of schools. There are many who claim, and the number is probably increasing, that the studies most needed as a preparation for college are precisely the studies most needed by those who have no inten-

tion of going to college.   It follows that the colleges and
universities are coming more and more to regard themselves as the natural continuation of the high school, in
much the same sense as the German university is the
natural continuation of the *Realschule* and the *Gymnasium*.
Under the impulse of this belief the chaos that has hitherto
prevailed in our educational methods is gradually giving
place to systematic organization, and we are coming to have
some approach to what may fairly be called an organic
educational system.

This tendency is unquestionably aided by the prevalent
system providing for the examination of high schools by
officers of the university.   This system, introduced by
Michigan nearly thirty years ago, has taken root in one
form or another in nearly every State.   The rigor with
which this examination is carried on varies greatly in
the several States.   In California, for example, the instruction in every study in every high school is inspected by a
professor especially qualified to judge of teaching in that
particular study, and such an examination is at present
insisted upon every year.   A report on the condition of the
school is made, not only to the university, but also to the
School Board.   Who can fail to see that such a system
must have a prodigious influence in elevating the pedagog-
ical standards of the secondary schools?   In other States
the system is less perfectly organized and perhaps less
perfectly administered, but in nearly or quite every State
some system of examination and articulation is established.

Perhaps it may not be out of place to say a word in regard to the practical question of method of support.   There
is considerable variety.   The public money that goes to the
high school in addition to the amount raised by local taxation is systematically provided for by the Legislature, and
is generally distributed on the basis of the number of pupils
in attendance at approved schools.   Standards are kept up
by official examinations provided for by the Department of
Education, as no public money is given to schools falling
below the standards required.

2

Methods of supporting higher education are still more variable. In a few of the States the universities are still dependent chiefly or entirely upon the amount received from the Federal Government and the more or less precarious annual or biennial legislative appropriation; but it is worthy of note that the tendency has set strongly in the direction of a permanent provision by taxation that may be relied upon year after year. The growth of this tendency may be illustrated by one or two examples.

In Michigan provision was made some thirty years ago for an annual tax of one-twentieth of a mill on every dollar. Supplementing this tax were specific appropriations for specific purposes. This method, however, was unsatisfactory, because of the embarrassing uncertainty of the university authorities in regard to the income that would be at their disposal. It soon came to be seen that nothing is more essential than stability of purpose; consequently, three years ago the policy was modified by lessening the number of specific appropriations and raising the amount of the annual tax to one-sixth of a mill upon the dollar.[1]

In Wisconsin, one-tenth of a mill was voted in 1876. A little later this amount was increased to one-eighth; in 1891 one-tenth of a mill was added for six years, but before the six years elapsed the tax was made permanent. In 1895 an additional tax of one-fifth of a mill was levied for two years, which, in turn, was made permanent in 1897. Thus the Legislature has provided for a permanent tax of 17-40 of a mill, which at presents yields an income of about $254,-000 a year. Besides this amount it turns over one per cent. of what is known as the railroad license income for the college of engineering; $12,000 a year for institute work, and certain other small sums for specific purposes. The total income from the State is somewhat more than $278,-000 per year. It need hardly be added that this amount is exclusive of the sums realized from the several Congressional grants, from bequests and from fees for tuition.[1]

[1] See p. 26.

Other illustrations might be given, but it is unnecessary, and I fear that I have already ventured into the domain of tediousness in the presentation of these concrete details. One or two brief considerations and I will relieve your patience.

In the States added to the Union since the beginning of this century, there is great variety of method, but there is always a remarkable uniformity of belief that higher education cannot be adequately provided for except by State support. Here and there, it is true, outcries are still heard against the system of taxation for high schools and universities, but such outcries seldom, perhaps I ought to say never, result in any change of policy. They sometimes, perhaps, modify or lessen the amount of appropriations for a time, but they add to the agitation of the subject, which, in the end, invariably strengthens the cause they were intended to defeat. Perhaps it ought to be said that another effect is to condemn the agitator to speedy political obscurity. An interesting monograph might be written to show that the most facile descent to political oblivion is the way that is ever kept open to him who achieves notoriety by attacking the State support of higher education. Not a few political aspirants in the course of the last fifty years have attempted this method of climbing into popular favor, but it would be difficult to name a single one whose political career long survived. They have either been converted or hopelessly lost. In the picturesque language of the region, "Such a man makes a good stranger." The people may submit to crudities and vagaries, but they will not tolerate attacks on what they persist in regarding as one of the most vital interests of the State. They not only reject the dogma that the common schools are enough, but they boldly proclaim and insist upon the doctrine that the welfare of the commonwealth demands the higher education of the few quite as much as the elementary education of the many.

Nor can it be successfully denied that the affairs of the

State University have, on the whole, been wisely, econo-
mically and successfully administered. That mistakes have
not sometimes been made, no reasonable man can assert,
but the privately endowed institutions also live in glass
houses. Everybody remembers the witticism of Mr. Evarts
in explaining why Washington was able to throw a silver
dollar across the Potomac. President Angell has said that
the University of Michigan has been able to make a dollar
go farther and bring back more than any other institution
in the country. The proud boast is justified by the remarkable history of that institution. Others have been
apt pupils and have caught the knack of similar success.
Boards of regents have come more and more to be wisely
organized and fewer and fewer mistakes have been made as
time has advanced. One doubt after another has died away,
and that confidence has gradually been established which is
now inviting and securing the union of private benevolence
and public support. As time progresses, the two methods
will more and more go hand in hand. It may confidently
be asserted that there is nothing whatever in the history of
State universities to prevent a happy marriage of the two
systems. Fortunate, indeed, is the university that can
bring to such a union the dower of a great name and a
great history; and still more fortunate is the commonwealth
which can have the opportunity of such an alliance.

STATISTICS ON STATE AID TO HIGHER EDUCATION.*

By St. George L. Sioussat.

The object of this statement is to show:

I. **What some of the States of the Union have appropriated in the last few years towards the support of their State Universities.**

II. **What help has been given by the State Legislatures to universities and colleges upon private foundations.**

III. **How some of the money for these purposes has been raised.**

IV. **What States exempt the property of educational institutions from taxation, and the extent of such exemptions.**

I. APPROPRIATIONS TO STATE UNIVERSITIES.

It will be convenient to consider these institutions in three groups:—1. State Universities of the South; 2. State Universities of the Middle West; 3. State Universities of the Far West.

In each of these groups *only the most important* will be selected for exemplification.

1. State Universities of the South.

University of Virginia and University of Texas.

University of Virginia.

Starting nearest home, we find that the University of Virginia has received from the State annual appropriations

---

* In these statistics, the figures for appropriations of early years are taken from Blackmar's Federal and State Aid to Higher Education (Bureau of Education: Contributions to American Educational History, No. 9.) The figures for recent years are taken from the Annual Reports of the U. S. Commissioner of Education, and from State Laws.

ever since its foundation in 1818. As the needs of the University have grown, the liberality of the State has increased, as may be seen from the following State appropriations:

1818-76 (except 1863-65), $15,000 per annum....			$825,000
1876-84,	30,000	"	240,000
1884-95,	40,000	"	440,000
1895-97,	50,000	"	100,000
1823 and 1884, special appropriations for buildings, etc.			122,000

Total State appropriations $1,727,000

1896-97, income of University from State appropriations	$50,000
income of University from all other sources	79,425

Total income $129,425

Besides appropriations to her University, Virginia has from early times appropriated something towards the support of the other colleges in her domain, such as William and Mary College, the Virginia Military Institute, etc. Her appropriations for these colleges (*i. e.* apart from the University) up to 1896 aggregated $849,500.

The entire sum of Maryland's appropriations to *all* the colleges within her borders is not more than $885,000, an amount about equal to Virginia's appropriations to colleges other than the University.

Although, according to the U. S. Census for 1890, the entire value of Virginia's real and personal property as assessed for taxation is $415,249,107, while that of Maryland is assessed at $529,494,777, Virginia has appropriated $1,700,000 more than Maryland for higher education, and has appropriated it to the leading institution in the State— the University of Virginia.

University of Texas.

After Texas became a State she reserved over 3,000,000 acres of public land for the foundation and support of a university. When it was found that the income from this land was inadequate to meet the growing needs of the institution, the State began a system of yearly appropriations, which aggregate $700,000. The largest annual grant (a special appropriation) was in 1892, when the University received $107,000
In 1894-95 income from State appropriation was.. 25,000
" 1895-96   "   "   "   "   "   75,000
" 1896-97   "   "   "   "   "   22,500

While these represent the more important of the Southern State Universities, they by no means complete the list. The University of Georgia, for instance, has received over $700,000 from the State; while South Carolina, with a taxable basis (Census of 1890) of $168,262,669, not one-third as large as Maryland's, has appropriated at different times to *four* colleges within her borders sums aggregating little less than $3,000,000, or more than three times as much as Maryland.

2. STATE UNIVERSITIES OF THE MIDDLE WEST.

The Universities of Indiana, Illinois, Michigan, Wisconsin, Missouri, Iowa, Minnesota, Kansas and Nebraska.

Introductory.—Those States whose domains were included in the Northwest Territory received from the United States, by provision of the Ordinance of 1787, the grant of two townships of public land, the proceeds of which were to be devoted to the establishment and maintenance of a seminary of learning. As the country farther West became settled and formed into territories, similar provisions and grants of land were made by the United States. The amount of the funds realized from the sale or lease of these lands varied directly with the care taken in the management and disposition of them. It is important, however, to note that in each State *some* proceeds were realized, which were devoted to a " Permanent Productive Fund " for the support of the State University. These national land grant funds were supplemented in some cases by private endowment, and in others by loans or gifts by the State of land or money for building. The interest from these permanent funds, the tuition fees (where such are charged), and the annual appropriation from the State are the three principal sources of income of the Western State Universities.

University of Indiana.

The State of Indiana in 1883, by legislative enactment, levied a tax for twelve years of one-half of one per cent on each $100 of the assessed valuation of the State. This was calculated to yield in twelve years the sum of $700,000, which was to be known as the " Permanent Endowment Fund of the University." Before this, there had been, from 1867-73, an annual appropriation of $8,000. This was increased in 1873 to $23,000. If to these appropriations we add special appropriations for buildings, etc., to the amount of $82,000, we get a grand total of $1,529,000 as Indiana's contribution to her University. The appropriation for 1896-97 was $80,000.

University of Illinois.

Illinois was for many years somewhat behind her neighbors in expenditures upon her State University. From 1869 to 1893 her entire appropriations aggregated only

$754,380

But in the years 1893-97 Illinois appropriated.... 744,666

Total appropriation $1,499,046

	Income from State Appropriation.	Income from all sources.
1893-94	$141,882	
1894-95	148,269	$244,677
1895-96	333,300	444,593
1896-97	121,215	226,592
	$744,666	$915,862

University of Michigan.

This institution has always been, and still is, one of the most influential of the universities of the Middle West. The cause of this superiority is twofold: (1) Able management for a long period of time; (2) ample support which the University has received from the State. In thirty years, from 1867 to 1897, the State appropriations to all the departments of the University have amounted to $3,018,047.

Below are given the appropriations for the last four years and the total income for the last three years:

Year.	Income from State Appropriation.	Income from all other sources.	Total Income.
1893-94	$250,000		
1894-95	231,722	$202,192	$433,914
1895-96	194,333	210,365	404,698
1896-97	197,000	224,635	421,635
	$873,055		

In the following table the figures in the *first* column represent the valuation of real and personal property as assessed for taxation in the States of Michigan and Maryland. The *second* column gives the income, from all sources *other* than State appropriation, of all the universities and colleges in the State (in Maryland, including the Johns Hopkins University), while the *third* column gives the State appropriations to all universities and colleges for the year 1895-96.

	Assessed Valuation.	Income from all sources except State.	State Approp'tion.
Michigan	$898,155,532	$367,913	$194,333
Maryland	529,494,777	234,462	20,575
Ratio of Maryland to Michigan	1:1.7	1:1.5	1:9.4

University of Wisconsin.

The total appropriations of Wisconsin to the State University aggregate $2,883,668.

The appropriations for the last four years follow:

Year.	State Appropriation.	Total Income.
1893-94	$276,095	
1894-95	274,150	$389,150
1895-96	282,000	400,000
1896-97	283,476	394,207

University of Missouri.

The University of Missouri has received altogether from the State $1,590,208. In 1892 was the largest single appropriation, $350,000.

Year.	State Appropriation.	Total Income.
1895-96	$77,577	$195,181
1896-97	66,318	183,777

University of Iowa.

Total State appropriations, $1,203,026. The largest single appropriation, that for 1891-92, was $90,500.

Year.	Income from State Appropriation.	Income from all sources.
1893-94	$67,000	
1894-95	68,354	$131,384
1895-96	65,500	138,003
1896-97	76,000	148,377

Assessed valuation of property, Iowa.........$519,246,110
    "   "   " Maryland..... 529,494,777

University of Minnesota.

Aggregate of State appropriations, $1,050,953.
Income from 1894 to 1897:

Year.	Income from State.	Total Income.
1894-95	$150,800	$284,457
1895-96	110,071	268,409
1896-97	82,333	284,091

University of Kansas.

Aggregate of State appropriations, $1,302,010.
Income from 1894 to 1897:

Year.	Income from State.	Total Income.
1894-95	$ 86,500	$ 95,500
1895-96	108,000	116,410
1896-97	100,800	109,020

	Assessment for Taxation.	Total State Aid.
Kansas	$347,717,219	$1,302,010
Maryland	529,494,777	885,000

University of Nebraska.

Aggregate of State appropriations, $1,645,456.
Special appropriations:

1891-92	$246,650
1893-94	118,170
1894-95	60,000
1895-96	63,572
1896-97	158,072

	Total Assessment for Taxation.	Total State Appropriation.
Nebraska	$184,770,305	$1,645,456
Maryland	529,494,777	885,000

3. STATE UNIVERSITIES OF THE FAR WEST.

University of California.

Aggregate of State appropriations, $1,901,702.
Income for 1893-97:

Year.	Income from State.	Income from all other sources.	Total Income.
1893-94	$120,137		
1894-95	119,825	$163,752	$283,577
1895-96	119,709	167,001	286,710
1896-97	177,761	161,090	338,851

Besides these appropriations, the State, in the early period of the University, donated certain swamp lands for the creation of a " Permanent Endowment Fund " for the University.

```
These lands sold for .................$  811,500
The income from this fund for 23 years, at
    $50,000 per annum, would be.....  1,150,000
                                     ─────────
                                     $1,961,500
State appropriations ................  1,901.702
                                     ─────────
                                     $3,863,202
```

Nearly four million dollars were contributed by California to her University for its foundation and income.

NOTE.—The *totals* or *aggregates* given above, with the exception of those of Virginia and Maryland, are in reality too small by amounts ranging from $10,000 to $50,000 or over.   The reason of this is the fact that no figures are to be obtained for 1891–92.

II.   STATE AID TO INSTITUTIONS UPON PRIVATE FOUNDATIONS.

A.   MASSACHUSETTS.

1. *Harvard University.*

Although very early the object of private benefaction, yet throughout the colonial period Harvard College was obliged to depend for assistance upon the appropriations of the General Court of Massachusetts.   These appropriations from 1636 to 1786 aggregated, roughly ....$115,797 [1]

By act of 1814 it was provided that ten-sixteenths of the bank tax, amounting to $10,000, should be paid annually to the college for a term of ten years, yielding in all the sum of............... 100,000

The State of Massachusetts contributed to the foundation, etc., of the Harvard Museum of Comparative Zoology (1859-74) 235,000

Other appropriations aggregated   99,000

Adding *land grants* to value of about............   46,000
                                                ─────────
    Grand total *circa*.......................$595.797

---

[1] A sum which in reality represents values at least ten times as great as it would to-day.

2. *Williams College.*

Beginning with land grants and part of a bank tax, the appropriations of the State of Massachusetts to Williams College aggregate $157,000.

3. *Massachusetts Institute of Technology.*

While not strictly speaking a college or university, this institute's great reputation warrants the following statement:

In 1888 the Massachusetts Legislature made a gift to the Institute of Technology of $200,000. In return, the Institute promised to found twenty free scholarships. For the year 1895-96 the income of the Institute was $290,187. In spite of this large income the expenses exceeded so much as to leave a deficit at the end of the year of $15,935.29. Upon application to the Legislature a grant was obtained last year (1896-97) of $25,000 per annum for six years, aggregating $150,000.

B. CONNECTICUT.

Yale University.

Like Harvard, Yale received constant support from the Colonial legislature. Appropriations took the form now of land grants, now of taxes on rum, etc., now of bills of credit. While it is impossible to estimate the present value of these appropriations exactly, if we say, roughly, about $122,500, this will probably be an undervaluation.

Besides the above, Amherst, Dartmouth, Bowdoin and others have received smaller sums from time to time.

C. NEW YORK.

1. *Columbia University.*

Columbia grew out of King's College. This was founded in 1754 under the royal government. After the Revolution the college was reorganized under the name of Columbia College. State appropriations to King's College and Columbia College aggregate $140,000.

2. *Union College.*

From the time of its first charter, in 1795, to 1804

State aid amounted to ....$ 78,112
Since then, by lottery grants, the State has given.. 280,000

Total grants $358,112

3. *Hamilton College.*

Founded 1812.   Total appropriation $120,000.

Other New York colleges which have received State aid are Geneva, Cornell, University of Rochester, etc.

D. PENNSYLVANIA.

1. *University of Pennsylvania.*

Penn's Grammar School (1697), the Friends Public School, Franklin's Academy, and the University of Pennsylvania represent one institution in several different phases of development.   Franklin Academy was chartered in 1753, and two years later was made a college.   In 1779 some of its officers were suspected of disloyalty and its charter was taken away.   After the Revolution a charter was granted to a new corporation with the title " University of Pennsylvania," and an annual appropriation was made.   In 1789, however, the old corporation was restored, and the two were amalgamated in the University of Pennsylvania.

Between 1789 and 1889 State appropriations for the assistance of the University amounted to $275,000.

Below are given the income from State appropriations for the last three years, the income from all other sources, and the total income.

Year.	Income from State.	Income from all other sources.	Total Income.
1894-95	$ 70,121	$339,255	$409,376
1895-96	24,606	402,064	426,670
1896-97	125,000	424,019	549,019

By act of the Legislature, approved July 29, 1897, appropriations were made for two years, beginning June 1, 1897, as follows:

1. For maintenance of patients in the University
    Hospital ....$ 50,000
2. For the general maintenance of the University, 100,000
3. For the general expenses of the University.... 50,000

      Total $200,000

                    or $100,000 a year.

2. *Lehigh University.*

This University was founded by Judge Asa Packer, and was chartered in 1866. The following is from the comments of the Governor, Daniel H. Hastings, in his executive approval of the bill appropriating $150,000 to Lehigh University for the two years beginning June 1, 1897:

" For twenty-six years the Packer endowment was amply sufficient to meet the current expenses of the institution. During the last four years, by reason of the Lehigh Valley Railroad stock, which constitutes the endowment, failing to pay dividends, the income of the University has been entirely cut off. The trustees and friends of the University, however, with confidence that the embarrassment is only temporary, raised from their own private funds a sufficient sum of money to continue the work. It has been made clear to me that the financial embarrassment of the University is merely temporary, and its managers have come before the General Assembly asking an appropriation of $200,000 to bridge over their difficulties. . . . After almost a generation of successful philanthropic work, this call for temporary aid appeals alike to the sympathy and patriotism of our people, and for these reasons I have been constrained to withhold executive approval from only one-fourth of the sum appropriated by the General Assembly."

The items were as follows:

1. For maintenance ....$100,000 } Approved.
2. For general expenses........ 50,000 }
3. For general educational purposes, 25,000 } Disapproved.
4. For special maintenance of plant, 25,000 }

      Total appropriation $150,000

III. HOW SOME OF THIS MONEY HAS BEEN RAISED.

Not to dwell upon the Massachusetts levy, upon each family, of one peck of corn or its equivalent for the support of Harvard College, we find that in this century many different methods of raising money have been employed. Bank taxes, lotteries and rents have furnished parts of many college funds. To-day two methods seem to be most favored:

(1) Provision for university appropriations in the general State budget.

(2) Special taxes, at given rates.

As examples of the first method we have Virginia, Pennsylvania, Massachusetts, and most of the older States.

As examples of the second method we have the Western States: Michigan, etc. This will require fuller mention.

Indiana, as was shown above, levied a tax in 1883 for twelve years of five mills on each $100 of taxable property, calculated to yield $700,000.

Michigan, during 1873-93, raised part of her appropriations by a tax of one-twentieth of a mill on each dollar of property. This was increased in 1894 to one-sixth of a mill, yielding about $150,000 per annum.

Minnesota in 1897 raised her former tax of fifteen-hundredths of a mill to twenty-three hundredths of a mill, causing a net increase of about $40,000 per annum.

Wisconsin, after raising her annual tax from one-tenth of a mill to one-eighth, in 1891 added a tax of one-tenth of a mill for six years. Before the six years had passed, this was made a permanent tax. In 1895 was levied an additional tax for two years of one-fifth of a mill. In 1897 this, too, was made permanent; so that at present there is a permanent tax of seventeen-fortieths of a mill, which yields annually about $254,000.

California up to this year levied a tax of one-tenth of a mill. For 1898 she has raised it to one-fifth of a mill. It is estimated that this will increase the appropriation by about $120,000.

IV. EXEMPTION FROM TAXATION.

1. *Constitutional* provisions for the exemption of educational property from taxation.

Colleges, universities and seminaries of learning are exempted from taxation by the Constitutions of the following States : Georgia,[1] Minnesota, Louisiana and South Carolina.

Any public property held for educational purposes is constitutionally exempted from taxation in Alabama,[1] Florida,[1] Illinois,[1] Indiana,[1] Kansas,[1] Nebraska,[1] Nevada,[1] North Carolina,[1] Oregon,[1] South Carolina,[1] Tennessee,[1] Virginia,[1] and West Virginia.

2. Provision by *statute laws* for the exemption of educational property from taxation:

(1) Productive property, or such as is held as an investment for the support of non-State schools, is exempt from taxation in the following States: Connecticut, Indiana, Kentucky, Louisiana, Maine, Minnesota, Mississippi, Nebraska, North Carolina, Oregon, Rhode Island, Tennessee, Vermont, Virginia.

(2) Unproductive property, or such as is invested in buildings, grounds, libraries, apparatus, etc., used and occupied exclusively for educational purposes by non-State schools, is exempt from taxation in the following States: Alabama, Arkansas, Colorado, Iowa, Kansas, Maryland, Massachusetts, Michigan, Missouri, Montana, Nevada, New Hampshire, New Jersey, New York, Ohio, Pennsylvania, South Carolina, Texas, Washington, West Virginia, Wisconsin.

(3) State in which all school property not belonging to State institutions is taxed : California.[2]

---

[1] In these States the Constitution provides, in each case mentioned, that the property referred to "may" be exempted from taxation ; in other States the declaration is imperative.

[2] These statements were taken from Blackmar's Federal and State Aid to Higher education.

ADDENDA.

TAXABLE BASIS, STATE APPROPRIATIONS AND TOTAL COLLEGE INCOMES.

	Value of property in State as assessed for taxation, Census of 1890.	Total of State appropriations 1895-96 to Universities and Colleges in the State.[1]	Total Income for 1895-6, from *all sources*, of all the Universities and Colleges in the State.[1]
New York	$3,785,910,313	$151,046	$2,576,396
Pennsylvania ...	2,659,796,909	335,740	1,603,436
Illinois	809,682,926	333,300	1,595,180
Ohio	1,778,138,477	185,785	1,059,363
California	1,101,136,431	119,709	628,091
Missouri	887,975,928	77,577	623,921
Michigan	898,155,532	194,333	562,246
Wisconsin	577,066,252	282,000	525,660
Indiana	856,838,472	40,000	436,060
Tennessee	382,760,191	20,600	434,143
Iowa	519,246,110	65,500	387,405
Minnesota	588,820,213	110,071	368,955
Virginia	415,249,107	65,500	340,292
Kansas	347,717,219	108,000	270,327
Texas	780,898,605	75,000	265,974
Maryland	529,494,777	20,575	255,037
Nebraska	184,770,305	63,572	235,547
Kentucky	547,596,788	35,556	215,209
Washington	217,612,897	70,000	126,305
Massachusetts ..	2,154,134,626		1,676,256
Connecticut	358,913,956		852,146
New Jersey	893,859,866		313,500

Massachusetts, Connecticut and New Jersey, the States in which are located the Universities of Harvard, Yale and Princeton, now give no regular or annual State aid.

---

[1] This of course excludes Normal Schools and all Institutions not giving the degree of Bachelor of Arts. The above figures are to be found in the U. S. Census for 1890 and the Report of the Commissioner of Education for the year 1895-6.

THE STATE UNIVERSITIES OF THE WEST

AN ADDRESS

BY

HON. JAMES B. ANGELL, LL. D.

President of the University of Michigan

DELIVERED AT THE SEVENTEENTH COMMEMORATION OF THE
JOHNS HOPKINS UNIVERSITY, FEBRUARY 22, 1893

You have enriched this day, long so dear and sacred to all Americans, with new and appropriate associations. When you decided to establish an annual festival on which to pay tribute to the memory of the founder of this great school of learning, and to confer together on some of the large problems of higher education, you were led by a happy inspiration to choose the birthday of Washington, not the least of whose titles to the affectionate regard of American scholars was his profound interest in advanced education. This he evinced in many ways, but especially by his generous efforts for the establishment of a national university.

In attempting to discharge the honorable duty to which I am now called, it has seemed to me that I should not be departing from the worthy traditions which dedicate this hour to the consideration of educational themes, if I should speak of the State universities of the West, their origin, their peculiar organization, the embarrassments they have experienced, the benefits they have conferred and their probable future.

The history of education in this country during the last
sixty years records no more striking phenomenon than the
rise and rapid growth of these universities in every State
from Ohio and Michigan on the east to California on the
west, and from the Dakotas on the north to Texas on the
south. Some of them are yet in a nascent stage of existence, because the States whose names they bear have only
just emerged from the territorial life. Others are fairly
started on a prosperous career, though many of the urgent
wants of a good college are still unsupplied to them. A few
have reached a development which entitles them to chal-
lenge comparison with the older and richly endowed institutions in the Eastern States, whether we consider the
number of their students, their educational appliances or
the ability of their faculties. That they should in half a
century or less have overtaken universities and colleges
which had been growing in the Atlantic States under auspicious circumstances for a century and a half or two cen-
turies is a fact of striking interest and importance. It
certainly merits the attention even of this section of the
country, in which the endowments of the higher institutions
of learning are furnished almost wholly by private beneficence. To travelers from the continent of Europe, where
the universities are all sustained by the States, it is the
organization of the Eastern, not that of the Western universities, which appears anomalous.

But although several of the colleges and universities in
the East, including Harvard and Yale and Williams and the
earlier collegiate institutions in Maryland and the Massachusetts Institute of Technology and all the agricultural
colleges, some of which are constituent parts of the old
classical colleges of New England and the Middle States,
have been aided by the States or by the United States or
by both, still, unless I am mistaken, there is a widespread
impression upon the Atlantic seaboard that the life of the
State universities of the West hangs on a very precarious
tenure, and that in spite of the fact that nearly every one

of them is growing with great rapidity and that every new State, on its admission to the Union, proceeds at once to organize its university, these institutions are destined to come to the ground in ruins. Pardon me for saying that these apprehensions are largely due to a lack of familiarity with State universities and with the laudable zeal of the West for higher education. Their history shows that they have had as natural and normal a growth as the endowed institutions of the East, that they are rooted in the very life and conditions of the people, and that though they must encounter obstacles, yet if they are conducted with discretion they have every prospect of a useful and successful future.

I. The State universities have a noble origin. They owe their birth to the inspiring command which rang forth from that great instrument that dedicated the Northwest forever to freedom, morality and intelligence, the Ordinance of 1787. While providing that the foot of no slave should ever curse the soil of that vast domain, from which five imperial States have been carved, it also declared, in words that are as familiar and as dear to the inhabitants of those States as the most precious words of the Declaration of Independence, " religion, morality and knowledge being necessary to good government and the happiness of mankind, schools and the means of education shall forever be encouraged."

The same spirit which led to the adoption of the Ordinance prompted Congress to make appropriations of lands at an early day for the establishment of a university and of schools in Ohio. And from that day to this every State which has been admitted to the Union has received a gift of lands for the endowment of a university. Congressmen from the East have united with Congressmen from the West in favoring this benign policy. If anything is settled by precedent, it is that the federal government is to encourage every new State to establish a university by an endowment of public lands. It is upon federal endowments that all the

State universities of the West have originally depended for
their maintenance. We can hardly suppose that the framers
of the Ordinance could have foreseen the far-reaching consequences of their action. It is doubtful if any statute was
ever passed in our history which will prove to have been
more fruitful of lasting good.

As the young universities grew, and the proceeds of the
national endowments proved insufficient to meet their
needs, the States were called on to assist. They have
made generous appropriations of money. Several of them
regularly levy a tax of a fraction of a mill on each hundred
dollars of property, and in addition at each session of the
Legislature raise a further sum of from $50,000 to $100,000
or more a year for the aid of their university. Michigan
has raised by taxation over $2,000,000 in all for her uni-
versity. The Wisconsin Legislature, in a recent session,
besides aiding in meeting the current expenses of the State
University, gave $300,000 for a science hall. When Mis-
souri received her portion of the direct tax, which Congress
refunded to the States, she devoted the whole sum, $646,000,
to her university. Private beneficence has also done not a
little to supplement the gifts of the States and the United
States. Kansas University has received a bequest of nearly
$200,000 from a citizen of Massachusetts. The University
of Minnesota has received a building costing $150,000 from
a citizen of Minneapolis. It must be admitted, however,
that for reasons which are obvious it has not been so easy
to procure large personal gifts for the universities which
can draw on the treasury of a Commonwealth as for those
which are wholly dependent on private endowments. But
there are cheering signs that the universities may hope to
fare better in this regard in the future than they have fared
in the past. It may be said with truth that few other
universities have had so large resources as they in the first
thirty or fifty years of their existence.

II. The organization and powers of the governing board
of the State University are determined by the constitution

of the State. The members of the board, usually styled
regents, are in some States appointed by the Governor, in
others elected by the people, and in yet others are State
officers acting *ex officiis* as regents. The boards are smaller
than the boards of trustees of endowed colleges, in Michigan, for instance, numbering only eight. They generally
serve for terms of six or eight years, though in Wisconsin
for a term of only two years. In Michigan the constitution
makes them a branch of the State government, removable
only by impeachment, and entirely independent of legislative control except in the use of funds specifically appropriated by the Legislature. In some States they are too
much under legislative control.

As no salary attaches to the office of regent, the position
is not much sought by mere politicians. The boards meet
with more frequency than the trustees of most endowed
colleges. Those of Michigan, for instance, meet monthly
or oftener. The number of members being small, each
feels a considerable sense of responsibility and, I think,
gives more attention to his duties than most trustees of
colleges. So far as I have observed, they are not often
affected in their official action by political bias. There
seems to be a growing tendency to put alumni upon the
boards. As the financial reports of the universities have to
be subjected to the scrutiny of the State auditor or treasurer,
an effective check is thus provided to malfeasance by the
financial officers of the university. On the whole, the
organization of the responsible governing bodies of these
State institutions is fairly satisfactory, though in some States
there is room for improvement.

III. I desire now to describe with the utmost frankness
some of the embarrassments to which they have been subjected.

1. In the first place most of them lost through unwise or
fraudulent management a large part of the national endowment. The lands were rented or sold at a great sacrifice
in early days when the public domain was apparently un-

limited, and when no one appreciated how great the needs of a university in our day would be. Shrewd speculators outwitted in some cases the lawful guardians of the university endowment. The story is not a cheerful one to dwell on. The institutions in the younger States have fared better in this regard.

2. The State universities, whose national endowment is not large enough to free them from dependence on legislative appropriations for support, have occasionally suffered from inability to secure continuity in some of their work. When a certain kind of instruction, for example in architecture or in medicine, had been begun under specific appropriations by one Legislature, it has subsequently been necessary to discontinue it because the next Legislature failed to continue the appropriation for that purpose. I need not say how serious such interruptions are, though, of course, through financial reverses they sometimes befall endowed colleges. The troubles of this kind are diminishing, because the life of each university is becoming more stable as the years go on, and the scope of the work it can wisely undertake is becoming more definitely recognized both by regents and Legislatures.

3. The State universities have had to contend against an earnest opposition on religious grounds. They have had to meet the charge that they are "godless institutions," and hence unfit homes for young men and young women during the period of their higher education. Many students have been turned aside from them by this charge, which has been made by two different classes—first, by those who maintain that a university supported by the State cannot tolerate, much less cherish, a Christian spirit in its teachers and pupils, and, secondly, by those who desire to build up denominational colleges at the expense of the State universities.

There can be no doubt that the majority of the parents who send their children to our higher institutions of learning would prefer that those children should find themselves

in circumstances friendly, rather than hostile, to the cultivation of a genuinely religious spirit and life. And most
of them have come to see that in the State universities the
conditions of life are not unpropitious to the development
of high moral and religious character. In them, as in all
American colleges, the teachers are, as a rule, men of sincere
Christian character, and are as free there as anywhere to
exert a legitimate influence in building up the spiritual life
of the students. Through the medium of voluntary associations, composed of teachers and students, there is abundant opportunity in every State university for the development of a sincere and deep spiritual life in one's self and
in others. There has been little or no complaint that professors in State universities were exerting a more positive
Christian influence than they ought. The great body of
people interested in higher education cherish in a more or
less generous sense the religious ideal of character, and will
not complain of the teachers who in a broad and unsectarian
way influence the young to attain to that ideal. The embarrassments of the State universities have come rather
from the lack of sympathy and co-operation of religious
people who, from a mistaken sense of duty or from misapprehensions of the spirit prevailing in such institutions, have
held themselves aloof from them. But an auspicious change
in the attitude of this class is going on. They are founding
religious halls in proximity to the universities, and through
guilds and other organizations are seeking to aid in the
cultivation of religious life among the students.

4. I think the State universities are often more exposed
than the endowed universities to unintelligent and mischievous criticism. This point is not due in any considerable degree to partisan interference with them. The public
schools and the State universities and agricultural colleges
have so strong a hold upon the public esteem that no party
and no party leader would find it profitable to make an
attack upon them. But critics and newspapers do feel, and
justly enough, somewhat freer to comment adversely upon

the administration of an institution sustained by the taxpayers than upon the conduct of one maintained by private
beneficence.   Harvard and Yale and Columbia do not, indeed, altogether escape the criticisms of editors and cor-
respondents.   But where differences of opinion have arisen
between members of the board of regents or members of the
faculties of State universities, more vehement and passionate
and unreasonable discussion than is common in the East
has sometimes flooded the newspapers of the West, because every taxpayer has a right to be informed concerning
the conduct of the institutions which he helps sustain.   This
has occasionally wrought incidental and temporary embarrassment, and has caused discomfort to faculties who were
subjected to unjust criticisms by scribblers entirely incom-
petent to pass judgment on university problems.   Still, it is
very proper that a State university should be open to public
criticism, and even a considerable freedom of comment has
the incidental advantage of directing general attention to the
institution and of awakening a certain public interest in it.
It is not altogether unwholesome for any of us who are
entrusted with the care of a university, whether trustees or
professors, to be held responsible in some degree to the
judgment of the public, which in the long run is not likely
to be unreasonable in its demands upon us.   But partisan
meddling with the Western universities has been far less
frequent than is generally believed in the East.

IV. Having now with the utmost frankness set forth the
embarrassments which State universities have encountered,
let me endeavor to describe with moderation the services
which they have rendered.

1. They have enabled one or two generations of men to
obtain a substantial collegiate or professional education
who otherwise must have been compelled to forego this
training, and they have furnished this supply of educated
men at the very time when the new States were urgently in
need of such leaders.   The Western States were settled by
men many of whom had received a collegiate education

in their native States in the East, and most of whom, whether college-bred or not, were fired with an intense desire to secure for their children the advantages of higher education.   But in their pioneer life it was absolutely impossible for them to send their sons east for collegiate training or to endow colleges at home.   When, therefore, Congress with singular prescience and statesmanship obeyed the mandate of the great Ordinance and gave public lands for the endowment of universities, these young States were enabled to offer to the settler the longed-for opportunities for his son to secure an education.   So from the cabins of logs and the huts of sods the boys, clad in the simplest garb, flocked to the unadorned halls of the new universities. So there was reared in the midst of the primitive life of regions just emerging from the condition of a wilderness a generation of men who in all the hot competitions and grave responsibilities of American life have shown themselves the peers of the most brilliant sons of the seaboard States and colleges.

One advantage of supreme worth to the West, and indeed to the whole country, the State universities have secured, in furnishing higher education, both collegiate and professional, almost without cost to the students.   The few rich men in that region could have sent their sons to Eastern colleges.   But, if their sons alone for the last generation could have enjoyed higher training, those new States would have been cursed with the social condition arising from having a small class of rich and educated men separated by a great gulf from the large class of poor and uneducated men.   As it is they have had hard problems enough, and still have them, in moulding the complex elements of their populations, drawn freshly from all parts of the world, into that social and political homogeneousness essential to the safe administration of republican institutions.   How much graver difficulty would they encounter if the poor had been excluded from the opportunities for education which have enabled many of them to rise to leadership in the social, political and religious life of those States in the formative period of their existence. The fathers did indeed build more wisely than they knew when they provided that as each Territory was born into Statehood it should have in its possession the germ of a university, which should grow with its growth and strengthen with its strength, and so furnish it with men equipped for all high public duties.

2. Again, the State universities have not only by their early organization been able to save a generation of educated men to the new States when those States particularly needed them, but they have also furnished a richer and more varied education than privately endowed colleges could have furnished before this time. It is only within the last few years that private beneficence has furnished an equipment for any college or university in the West at all comparable to the equipment of several State universities. This fact was due to no lack of generosity on the part of western men, but the exigencies of life in the young States were so pressing that large funds could not be released by business men for the ample endowment of great schools of learning. Most of the denominational colleges, worthy as is the work they have done with limited means, were compelled to confine their work within rather narrow limits. But the State universities were enabled at an early day to undertake varied scientific teaching, which is the most costly of all teaching, to gather pretty good libraries and to establish schools of law, medicine, dentistry, pharmacy and engineering. This breadth and variety of work have been impossible until very recently for any privately endowed school. How valuable the provisions for these different kinds of instruction have been to the West I need hardly say. Still further, the excellence which the resources of the States have enabled their universities to attain in the quality of their instruction has stimulated and compelled all the other colleges and universities to bring their work up to a higher standard than they could otherwise have attained, and so has lifted the grade of education through the West.

A good illustration is afforded, if I may without presumption speak of it, in the action of the University of Michigan in raising the standard of medical education by leading the way in extending its two courses of six months each to two of nine months, then to three years of nine months, and finally to four years of nine months, with a preliminary examination equal to that required for admission to the scientific department of American colleges. The best schools must follow, as indeed some are following, or lose their most aspiring students.

3. I ought, in justice to our ideas in the West, to say that we reckon among the advantages of our universities the fact that without exception they are and have been open to women. I do not propose to discuss here the question of co-education. But one can hardly overrate the blessings the State universities have conferred, not only on the women who have had the same training as the men, but also on the whole system of education in the West, by enabling the women, to whom so much of the teaching in western high schools is confided, to carry into those schools as good educational attainments and ideals as the men, and by delivering the West almost entirely from that most worthless of all educational shams, the old-fashioned female seminary, in which the most shallow and insipid instruction was given within those narrow limits beyond which it was not deemed possible, or at any rate prudent, for the mind of a young woman to be carried.

4. The State universities have wielded a most powerful influence for good by working in hearty co-operation with the public school system. This is relatively a matter of more consequence in the West than it would be in the East. A well-conceived and well-organized system of public schools comprising all grades, from the primary to the high school, was so early well established, partly on endowments of public lands, that outside of Ohio nearly all of the secondary education, including the preparatory training for college, is given in the high schools. It is easy to see why

the universities, supported like the schools by public funds, should naturally and readily come into relations with the schools which should prove mutually beneficial. Neither the denominational colleges in the West nor those in the East have succeeded like the State universities in coming into close and friendly contact with the high schools and in reaching through them the whole system of lower schools. This has been accomplished by various means, perhaps by none so efficiently as through the system of visitation and inspection of the high schools by members of the university faculty, with a view of receiving graduates into their classes, as the German universities receive students from the gymnasia. I do not propose to discuss that custom now. But whatever may be said of it, this certainly must be conceded, that it has furnished a great stimulus to the schools, has strengthened local pride in them, has improved the quality of instruction, has kindled in many a youth an ambition which he otherwise might never have felt to obtain a college education, has led these schools in some States in twenty years to push up their grade of work a full year, has kept the university in touch with them and has secured a real, where there was no formal, unity of organization in State systems of education from the primary school up through all the departments of the university. The lifting and inspiring power of the university is felt down through all the grades of the most elementary class in the lowest schools. This is a public service which cannot well be overestimated, and which probably could never have been rendered in equal measure in any other organization of the higher education. It is of vast consequence that the teachers, from the women in the kindergarten up through the primary and secondary schools and the college and the university, should all feel that their work is one, and should be drawn together by bonds of sympathy, of mutual appreciation of each other's work, and of a spirit of hearty co-operation for the same great end. Such an alliance imparts zest and pride to every teacher from the lowest to the highest, and strength and beauty to the whole educational system of a State.

V. And now what is to be the future of the State universities?   As their wants increase, can the States be expected to provide for them?   I cannot but be hopeful for
their future.   Like all other universities they will probably
not have all the means they could well use, much less all
they desire.   A university which has all it wishes has
already ceased to advance or begun to decline.   If it is not
reaching out for something better and larger than it has
obtained, the seeds of decay are planted within it.   If the
day ever comes when my friend, your President, does not
wish something more for this University than it has, then
I shall believe that the University has begun to die at the
roots, or if he will allow me to say it, that it is time for the
President to resign.   But that the States will enable their
universities to go on in a path of improvement at a reasonable pace I confidently expect.   They are under pledge to
the general government, from whom they have accepted
lands for the establishment of the universities.   They have
in most cases already a large amount of money, which they
cannot sacrifice, invested in the plant.   They cherish a pride
in the usefulness and reputation of these institutions.

Each State whose university has been in existence for
some years has within its borders so many of the graduates,
a considerable proportion of whom are persons of influence,
that public opinion would condemn any proposition to
abandon the principal school of learning.   The tendency of
late years has been to enlarge rather than diminish the
appropriations for the support of universities.   The States
seem to have settled on the policy of maintaining them, with
almost as little discussion as is evoked by the passage of
bills for the support of the State charitable institutions.
Like a privately endowed university they will doubtless
have their times of financial trials and disappointment.   But
the trend of the public sentiment for the last twenty years,
and the study of all the conditions of the life of the universities, justify the faith that, as the Commonwealths of
the West grow richer and more populous, they will provide

yet more liberally than they have provided in the past for their institutions of higher learning. It must be remembered that nearly every Western State has the territory and the resources of a European kingdom. Germany has a university for each two millions of her inhabitants. Ohio, Illinois, Indiana, Michigan, Missouri and Texas have each more than that number of inhabitants now, and other Western States will soon exceed it. Each may well have one large university within its borders, and all the signs indicate that in almost every Commonwealth the State university will be the great university, if there is to be but one.

You in the East often speak with a certain admiration of the unparalleled material development of the West, and predict that by virtue of the increase of its population that section will control the political destinies of the country. But, believe me, we in the West are sincerely striving to make the development of our schools, from the humblest to the highest, keep pace with the development of our abundant material resources. We hope that we are not unmindful of the fact that intelligence and character ought to outweigh, and often do outweigh, mere numbers in influence on public opinion. We know that we ought not to aspire to the shaping of the fortunes of the republic unless we can rear and place in power large-souled and broad-minded statesmen of whose leadership the whole nation may justly be proud.

We are seeking in our way to accomplish by our great schools what you in the East have so well accomplished chiefly by other methods than ours of sustaining such schools. We believe that in none of its educational work has the West shown more originality and more wise improvement of great opportunities than in the nurture of its universities. We have now reached a stage in our history where we can possibly combine your method of support with ours. We certainly have no scruples about accepting private gifts to supplement the generosity of the States. There are not wanting indications that we may expect them.

I have sometimes asked, also, whether as the wants of
your worthy Eastern universities grow more pressing and
their immeasurable blessings to their States and to the
nation become more and more obvious, these rich Eastern
Commonwealths will not imitate the examples of the fathers, and once more render aid to some of these great
schools. When one sees, for instance, what this university
in its brief life has already achieved for Baltimore and for
Maryland, as well as for the whole land, when one con-
siders that it has done a work which for amount and excellence seems to the sister universities out of all proportion to the means at its command, and has had a success
altogether unique in training men to take places in college
faculties, when one remembers that the provision made for
its support by its munificent founder, though it was deemed
very large fifteen years ago, no longer ranks as such by
the side of the incomes of some of those universities with
which alone the Johns Hopkins University should be compared, a Western university officer, accustomed to call on
his State for help, may be pardoned for suggesting the
inquiry, whether this proud and flourishing State of Maryland might not well do on a larger scale for this university
what she did in her earlier years on a smaller scale for St.
John's College and the University of Maryland, and what
her neighbor, Virginia, has done for her famous university,
even in the stress of poverty and war.

But of one thing I am sure, with whatever differences of
organization the universities of the West and the universities of the East may attempt to discharge their high duties,
they will cherish the most fraternal spirit toward each other
and bid each other God speed in their great work of pro-
moting sound learning in this nation.

In this spirit I have come to you on this your festal day
to bring you from the Western universities their salutations,
their congratulations, and their best wishes for the ever-
increasing prosperity of this renowned institution.

A CITY UNIVERSITY

AN ADDRESS

BY

HON. SETH LOW, LL. D.

President of Columbia College

DELIVERED AT THE NINETEENTH COMMEMORATION OF THE
JOHNS HOPKINS UNIVERSITY, FEBRUARY 22, 1895

It is the glory of Baltimore that here was illustrated for
the first time, in a new way, the availability of an American
city to be the home of a university. It is the glory of this
university that, being of a type new to American experience,
its methods and its ideals have been largely adopted by
both the older and the new institutions of the higher learning in the United States. I do not forget that my own
Alma Mater, Columbia College, had been at work in New
York for more than a century before the Johns Hopkins
was founded, nor that she wore the aspect of a university
in that she had surrounded herself even then with a series
of professional schools that already had a national reputation. Neither do I overlook the fact that, as early as 1857,
the Trustees of Columbia College endeavored to develop in
New York instruction of a university grade and spirit in
the subjects usually included in the faculty of philosophy—
in those subjects, in a word, which the Johns Hopkins has
made its own. But in 1857 neither time nor place were
friendly and the project failed of success. Naturally, I am
not speaking now of college work, for Columbia's contributions to the country on that side are neither few nor
small. When, therefore, President Gilman was called to

the duty of organizing the Johns Hopkins University, the man and the opportunity for a university of a new type met in America for the first time. The time at last was ripe, and the sagacious administrator was at hand to summon its possibilities into being. I trust that I shall not offend the sensibilities of the people of Baltimore if I say that, before the Johns Hopkins University was established, the city had no especial reputation as an educational centre. There must, indeed, have been here, in at least one mind, a clear apprehension of the great value to a community of an institution of the higher learning, or the foundation provided by Johns Hopkins would not have been set up. Today your city has both a national and an international reputation as the seat of this university. I marvel at the achievement of less than twenty years. If any argument were needed to demonstrate the fitness of a city to be the home of a university, your experience would supply it. I wonder if the people of Baltimore are alive to the fame that is theirs by reason of the work that the Johns Hopkins University has done in their midst. The city ought to cherish the university as the apple of its eye. No wealthy Baltimorean should die without adding to its resources. The name, like those of John Harvard and of Eli Yale, in time will become impersonal, and yours will be the pride and the enjoyment of its growing repute.

If I were to try to point out what this Baltimore university has done for the higher education in the United States, I should emphasize, first of all, the value of its demonstration that a university does not consist of great buildings, nor of an extensive campus, nor of any of the accessories which we have been in the habit of associating in these later years with our historic colleges. The university consists of its teachers, and of the libraries, the museums, the collections, the apparatus that is necessary for its work. Only this, and you may have a university. This is not to say that a university ought not to be nobly housed. If this were so, I should not be striving at this

moment to move the university of Columbia College to a
new site, the cost of which for land alone is $2,000,000.
When the conditions favor, a city cannot give to its university too noble a home. You may judge a city, indeed,
as to the estimate it puts upon the value of the higher learning, by the home it provides for its university, when the
university has brought to the city fame and the world's
regard. But, if President Gilman had used up his endowment in the construction of great buildings, men might,
indeed, have said, " behold, what great buildings are here,"
but they would not have said, as they now say, " behold,
what a university is here." I have ventured to adapt the
spirit of this illustration to my own work in New York.
I have urged the Trustees to put their own resources into
education, in the confidence that, when Columbia was seen
to be of increasing service to the city, the generous people
of New York would see to it that we should not go without
buildings. This policy, and this alone, in my judgment,
has made possible our recent development and has made
practicable our project of removal to the new site. It has
brought to Columbia College, in one way and another,
about $5,000,000 in five years.

This statement, in turn, helps to illustrate what we are
talking about when we speak of a city university. For the
work of an American college, in the historic sense, no such
vast endowments are necessary. It is true that the use of
the elective system and the teaching of natural science in
our colleges by laboratory methods call for larger endowments than were formerly sufficient, but the vast sums
needed by a university are not needed by a college even
now. The aim of the college is to give a liberal education.
It opens up vistas in many directions into wide domains of
knowledge, but it does not undertake to lead the student far
along any one path. It deals with students in considerable
groups, and withal, with students for the most part from
sixteen to twenty years of age. The university, on the
other hand, deals with students, for the most part, who are

upwards of twenty years of age. Ideally, these students have already had the liberal education which the college aims to supply. They are ready, therefore, to enter upon advanced work, and what they demand of the university is the opportunity to carry their studies in any direction which is of interest to the human mind to the utmost limit of that which is already known. They demand more than this. They wish to be taught how to make researches on their own account, how to use the books, the methods and the apparatus which make a man competent to add to the sum of human knowledge by contributions of his own. It is true that not every student who studies with that hope has the natural gifts to enable him to become an original investigator. On the other hand, students who pursue their studies by that method, at the very least become thoroughly acquainted with their subject as they cannot become acquainted with it in any other way. A necessary consequence of this aim of the university is to compel the university to deal with its students to a much greater extent as individuals. Each man must be guided in his reading and his experimental work as nearly as possible with the same care that would be bestowed upon him if the university had only a single student. It is an axiom in educational work that the higher the grade of such work, the greater the cost per capita. It costs less per capita to maintain the primary schools than the grammar schools, less per capita to maintain the grammar schools than the high schools, less per capita to maintain the high schools than the colleges, and very much less per capita to maintain the colleges than the universities. At every stage the causes that produce the increase of expense are the same, and they work with increasing force the higher one proceeds in the scale. Broadly stated, they are, as has already been indicated, that the range of studies open to the student body increases as the student advances on his path, and that the demands of the student upon the teacher call constantly for a higher grade of work and for more individual work. In addition to these two causes, there is, as one approaches the university, an increasing necessity for large outlay for apparatus. It may easily cost as much to carry on a single research in physics that will be conducted by one or two men as to provide laboratory instruction in physics for a large school of boys. A college needs a good reference library and a collection of standard books as large as may be readily had. It does not need a library for historical research nor for philological study, nor in general the exhaustive collections of books that become immediately important in any subject the moment even a single student undertakes to pursue his topic with the thoroughness of a trained investigator. How much it can cost to provide such opportunities in even a single line of study may be easily understood. When it is recalled that the duty of a university is to afford such opportunities around the whole circle of human knowledge, the mind is prepared to appreciate how very costly such an enterprise must be.

Thus far I have been dealing simply with the material side of the question. It goes without saying that a great investigator cannot be trained by things alone. He must come into contact with the spirit of research embodied in a living man. Such men, for the most part, are the ablest men to be found among the ranks of teachers. Ordinarily, they can command the highest salaries. In these days, a larger number of men are needed to cover thoroughly any one of the great fields of knowledge than was the case a generation ago. The tendencies that have shown themselves in the industrial world in the minute division of labor, in the scholarly world have revealed themselves no less strikingly in the direction of specialization. No one man, therefore, is any longer an authority on the whole of a great subject. For example, it is rare to find a man who is at the same time an acknowledged authority on the philology and on the literature of any one of the great languages. In the days when philology was less developed, it was easy for a

man to deal with the literature of a language and also satis-
factorily enough with the language itself. In our day it is
not so, and in my observation, at least, the characteristics
of mind which lead a man to take deep interest in philological questions are distinctly unfriendly to what may be called
the natural and spontaneous enjoyment of the literary pro-
ductions of the languages, such as any man who is able
to read is capable of responding to.   This, however, is only
by way of illustration.   The fact is undisputed that a university, in order to respond to the reasonable demands of
advanced students in these times, must ordinarily provide
not one man only, but several men, in order to secure adequate treatment of all sides of any great department of
knowledge.   No such comprehensive attitude towards literature or science or philosophy is expected of a college.
On the other hand, the university in which such privileges
cannot be had is still short of the ideal.

This leads me to say a few words in further explanation
of my conception of a university, for it must be admitted
that in our American usage of the word, it does not stand
for anything capable as yet of explicit definition.   This is
the less remarkable because it means a different thing in
England from what it means in France, and a different
thing in France from what it means in Germany and in
the other countries of Europe that have adopted the German conception and model.   I have said enough already
to make it clear that the university, in the sense in which
I have been speaking of it, is a comparatively new thing in
the United States.   It is natural, therefore, that even among
educators, the word should have an uncertain significance,
until with the lapse of time a common usage has been developed.   It is well understood that the American college
was, in its origin, the child of the English college.   The
different conditions to which it has been exposed have
modified the American college so that it is no longer exactly
like its prototype.   Nevertheless, in aim and in essence it
is the same thing, a school for liberal education.   The Eng-

lish university is a collection of English colleges. Its educational relation to the colleges is not greatly felt on the side of instruction. There are indeed a few university lecturers whom members of the colleges may listen to if they desire, but, for the most part, the instruction is given in the colleges and very largely by individual tutors. The university conducts the examinations and grants the degree, and thus, as it were, establishes the educational standard and places upon those who obtain the degree the imprimatur of the university. The educational aim, however, is not changed because the degrees are given by the university rather than by the separate college. This is the English conception of a university. It is said, and with some reason, I think, that the present educational system of France, which dates from the first empire, was modeled after that which was ideally outlined in New York by the law establishing a University of the State of New York. This law was largely the product of the constructive genius of Alexander Hamilton. I do not know that the accuracy of this inference is susceptible of proof. It is said, nevertheless, that the law establishing the University of France, and declaring its relations to the educational system in France, is so like the law framed by Hamilton and his colleagues that it is difficult to escape the conclusion that the author of the French law was at least familiar with the New York law. Only, in France, the law has been carried into active and efficient operation with all the authority of government behind it. In the State of New York it has remained practically a dead-letter. By this scheme all the educational institutions in the country are made a part of the University of France, just as in the State of New York it is theoretically the case that all the institutions of the higher learning are made a part of the University of the State of New York. But in New York the theory has not been felt in practice and each institution has worked out its own salvation as best it might. This, then, is the French conception of a university. Thus it is clear that the university about which

I have been talking is neither the English conception of a university, nor the French, even though the French conception exists in counterpart by statute in the laws of the State of New York. The result both of the English and of the French system has been to lead to the development of literature and scientific research chiefly outside of the universities. In Germany, on the other hand, we find a university system developed which has brought the student into close personal contact with the profoundest scholars of the country and the leaders of research in all directions of study. Thus the future teachers of Germany, and the future practitioners in all the learned professions as well, get their instruction and their preparation for their future work in an atmosphere as friendly as possible to the most thorough mastery of their own specialty and as friendly as possible to the development of original thinking and work upon their own part. This, I conceive, is the result that ought to be aimed at in the development of the American university. Naturally, the American university will not be exactly like the German university in all its details. It will have no such relation to the government, on the one hand, nor any such relation to the school system of the country, on the other. It will relate itself to the American college, which is an institution entirely American in its character-istics and as necessary and useful to-day as it ever has been in the long history of the country. Nevertheless, the aim which the German university has set before itself and which it has very largely realized under the conditions natural to German life, is the aim, in my judgment, which the Amer-ican university also should set before itself and which it must realize under the conditions natural to American life, because, after all has been said, the world is ruled by its thinkers, and civilization is carried forward by the patient investigators of natural laws; the lives of men are largely shaped by the teachings of experience as revealed by his-torical study; and the literature of men is enriched by every addition to our knowledge of the literature and language of the past. Nature's craftsmen in all these directions will produce results according to their gifts outside of a university if they get no opportunity within it. But the history of Germany clearly shows that the opportunity to serve mankind along such lines is much enlarged, if to train such men is the chosen aim of the university; in part, because in that case, the university affords the material apparatus by the aid of which the natural thinker or investigator can best do his work, and, most of all, because in a university so constituted, the atmosphere of the place and the spirit of the men who work there are friendly to such labors.

I am ready now to point out what I conceive to be the second great service which the Johns Hopkins University has done for the higher education in the United States. The American college has not itself made great scholars, for that was not its aim. It has, however, produced sound scholarship up to a certain point, and it has awakened in many a desire for more learning than the college itself could satisfy. Such students, in large numbers, during the last half-century have gone to Europe to complete their studies. It is noticeable that they have gone in a far larger stream to Germany than either to England or to France. This circumstance demonstrates, I think, that it is in Germany that the need is best met which Americans feel who desire to be thorough scholars and to become masters of their subject. The Johns Hopkins University set itself to demonstrate that such opportunities could be given in the United States by an institution deliberately adopting that aim and conducting its work with reference thereto. The older American colleges, like Harvard and Columbia, were in no way blind to the necessity of providing such opportunities. As I have already intimated, as early as 1857 the Trustees of Columbia College endeavored to make a movement in that direction. They were ahead of the times, however, at that date, and furthermore, they were embarrassed by the difficulty of adding to an educational establishment that had grown up with other aims a

new something that should represent this different ideal.
It is the glory of the Johns Hopkins University, as I conceive, that you perceived not only that the new departure
was timely, but also that a new institution was better able
to make it than any of the older ones. The work of the
Johns Hopkins University has been so successful that, by
slow degrees and after much effort, several of the older
foundations, and among them Columbia, are working now
with the same aim as distinctly and as intelligently as your-
selves.

The problem at such a university as Columbia is a very
different one from yours in Baltimore. In the conception
of a German university, all knowledge is comprehended in
four faculties—the faculty of theology, the faculty of medicine, the faculty of law and the faculty of philosophy. It
is clear at a glance that the first three faculties are faculties
that train men for the learned professions. The scope of
each one is roughly indicated by its name. The faculty of
philosophy includes all other knowledge—philosophical,
linguistic, scientific, historical, and the like. The Johns
Hopkins University, having its opportunity to choose, has
established here, in the first instance, a faculty of philosophy. It did not pretend to cover the whole of the field
covered by the faculty of philosophy in such a university,
for instance, as that of Berlin. It did aim to cover well
whatever portion of the field it entered into. That has
been its wisdom and the chief reason, I think, of its acknowledged success. Very recently it has begun to offer
instruction on the scientific side of medicine in connection
with the Johns Hopkins Hospital, which is now in operation. You will perceive that behind the university's instruction in medicine there is the same purpose of developing a scientifically trained student, so that the practitioner
shall be not merely a good practitioner, but a thoroughly
trained student in his profession. Having the opportunity
to start afresh, the Johns Hopkins University has wisely,
I think, placed its medical school upon a university basis

by demanding a college education as a pre-requisite for admission. This is not to say that a good doctor cannot be made without a college education, but it is to say that the duty of the university to the medical profession is not fully performed until it stands firmly, first of all, for a broadly developed man, and then for a broadly developed man scientifically trained in all matters pertaining to his profession. It is clear that, if the Johns Hopkins University will adhere to this wise policy, it will one day develop a university as nearly complete as the means at its command will permit and as American conditions will sustain.

I do not know to what extent the theological faculty will become a part of our American universities. More and more I expect to see the theological schools affiliated to the universities by some such system as prevails, for instance, at Columbia. But I do not yet foresee the time when theology can be studied in this country with the same spirit of free inquiry as American public sentiment supports in relation to medicine, law and general knowledge. At Columbia, Dr. Hastings, the President of the Union Theological Seminary, sits in our University Council, without a vote, but with the privilege of the floor, by virtue of an arrangement under which the educational opportunities of both institutions, where they touch each other, are made available for a single fee to the students of each. Arrangements somewhat similar in character, though less complete, exist between Columbia College and the General Theological Seminary (Episcopal) and the Jewish Theological Seminary as well. By such an arrangement as exists with the Union Theological Seminary, the university obtains the advantage of the theological point of view in shaping its educational policy; it contributes to the scholarly equipment of many students of theology, and obtains for its own students the privilege of attending, as electives, such courses in the theological seminary as may appeal to them. Both libraries, also, are open to the students of each institution on the same terms. In the meanwhile, the university

escapes all the controversies which at one time or another
are apt to show themselves in connection with theological
education. The plan also is adaptable at large. The same
university can, if it wishes, enter into the same arrangements
with more than one seminary.

At Columbia the historic American college had surrounded itself with professional schools in medicine, law
and applied science before the new ideal peculiar to the
university, as I have outlined it, became a recognized part
of its polity. Our undertaking, therefore, is not simply to
create, but also to transform. We do not desire to destroy
the historic college which has contributed so many famous
names to American history and whose endowments are the
basis of all the university development that Columbia can
command. We do, however, desire to relate the college to
the university in such a way as to benefit the college work
proper and the university work which is to follow it,
whether under the faculty of philosophy or under any of
the professional faculties. We do desire further to lift, as
we can, the standard of instruction in the professional
schools, until at last they shall all be upon a university
plane. For such a problem as this, time is as evidently
necessary as in the working out of your own problem, and
money, also, in untold sums, is essential before a satisfactory
result can be reached.

That is one reason why I think that both the Johns Hopkins and Columbia are fortunate in being located in cities.
Men who are able to give freely for education, as a rule,
are much more likely to give with an open hand to an
institution that they see and an institution which reflects
credit, or even glory, upon the city in which they live, than
they are to give to educational institutions at a distance, of
which they know little except by the hearing of the ear.
So far as educational benefactions come from men who are
themselves college-bred men, their gifts are not unlikely to
go to their Alma Mater; but it is an interesting circumstance that men who have not themselves enjoyed the

privilege of education are at least as likely as others to
establish great educational foundations. Such men, more
and more, I believe, will give to the institutions in the cities
that have this new aim, and to the university of their own
city in particular. I may be reminded that a citizen of
New York has been the largest contributor to the University of Chicago. This is true, but, so far as it traverses
my argument, it may be safely said to be an exceptional
case. In the meanwhile, these splendid gifts are developing
a university on the right lines in the great inland city of the
Union. Already that city has met the gifts from outside,
large as they have been, dollar for dollar within the city,
and one need not be a prophet nor the son of a prophet to
be confident that, among the universities of the country
dependent upon private foundations, none are more sure of
support from the wealth of the city about it than the University of Chicago. I like to think that the same thing is
true of Columbia College. It stands in the midst of the
greatest accumulation of wealth to be found in the country,
and this wealth is largely in the hands of generous givers.
The university has only to deserve support at the hands of
the city in order to receive it. The same thing ought to be
true *pro tanto* of the Johns Hopkins University. Baltimore
is not so large or so wealthy a city as either New York or
Chicago, but nevertheless it is a historic city, an important
city, and a wealthy city. Already the Johns Hopkins University has shown what can be accomplished with the gift
of a single citizen of Baltimore. When the city of Baltimore takes this university to itself and makes its renown a
matter of civic pride, then the Johns Hopkins University,
like these others, can expand its work to the full measure
of the opportunity afforded to it by the city.

But cities contribute to universities factors of the utmost
value other than direct gifts. I doubt a great deal, for example, whether the Johns Hopkins University could have
made the name it has if the Peabody Library had not been
at its service during all these years. The great libraries to

be found in cities, accessible to the competent student, are important contributions to the successful work of a university. Museums of all kinds may be made to contribute to its efficiency. In New York, for example, Columbia gives courses of public lectures on art every winter at the Metropolitan Museum of Art, using, as far as possible, the objects to be found in the Museum by way of illustration. At the American Museum of Natural History Columbia gives public lectures every winter on scientific subjects. Both of these institutions in return place their entire collections at the service of professors and competent students of Columbia for investigation and research. Columbia thus is able to avail itself of artistic and scientific collections that could not be acquired directly for the university without an outlay of many millions of dollars. In the meanwhile, by this relation to the Museums, Columbia adds to the public collections both a greater popular value and a greater scientific value. Its public lectures enable the people to understand and appreciate the collections in the Museums better than they otherwise could, while its use of the collections for investigation and research adds to their scientific value. Columbia College has similar relations with the Cooper Union, maintaining there every winter a series of lectures open to the public. These lectures are delivered in courses and are intended for instruction rather than for amusement. The Cooper Union, from the nature of the case, is unable to give anything in return except that it gives the room without charge. But Columbia believes that it is discharging a legitimate part of the work of an American university when it brings to the public the opportunity of hearing competent people on scientific, historical, economic and literary subjects. It is, if you please, simply the old Lyceum lecture delivered in courses; but it is also more than that, for it makes the people of the city of New York appreciate that the university is of consequence to them as well as to the comparatively few who are enrolled among the ranks of its students. The opportunities in every city for such alliances between the university and other institutions of a public character in the city are always numerous, and, in some cities, they are almost limitless. I believe it to be, from every point of view, sound policy for the university to welcome these alliances rather than to hold aloof. The American problem is not the German problem. The German universities are able to pursue their aim with the authority of the State behind them. Further than this, the learned professions and the profession of teaching are open only to graduates of the university. In the United States, the universities that are the most highly developed do not have the authority of the State behind them, neither do they hold exclusive command of the portals that open into the profession of the teacher or into any of the so-called learned professions. While, therefore, the American university should set before itself, as I think, the same aim which has made the German university so powerful an instrument for the service of humanity, the American university must nevertheless realize this aim under conditions that are very different. Our endeavor must be to offer opportunities for costly research, which, from the nature of the case, can be availed of directly by only a few students out of a vast population, and this we must do in the midst of a democratic community. A democratic community naturally believes in education, and to that extent our environment is favorable, but a democratic community is tempted to draw the line in education at the point where the masses are seen to profit by it. Therefore I am of the opinion that if our universities expect permanently to maintain the sympathy of the people in the developments upon which they have recently entered, they must, for their part, demonstrate to the people that this sort of study by the few is, without doubt, of the utmost service to the multitude. Such a faculty of philosophy as you have established in Baltimore becomes the natural school for teachers in the colleges and the high schools of the country. Even in Germany, they speak of the faculty of philosophy as the professional school for teachers. It is remarkable to what an extent the Johns Hopkins University has already fulfilled this function. This sort of service, I am sure, the people of the United States are able to understand; but it will also be wise for the universities, I am confident, to enter into as close practical relations with the life of the cities in which they may be located as the circumstances of each case permit. When I dream of Columbia and its possibilities, I always think of a university not only great enough to influence the life of New York, but of a university able to influence the life of New York because it is itself a part of it, and therefore able to understand it and to minister to it. Time would fail me were I to attempt to point out the many lines upon which a city university can come into helpful contact with the life of the city. I am persuaded that each university should study its own problem. It is no longer possible, if it ever was, for any one university to be foremost around the whole circle of human knowledge. The same university will excel at different times in different departments, but if a university strives to absorb that which is characteristic in the life of the city in which it does its work, I am persuaded that every city university will have a flavor of its own that will draw to it persistently the men who want that thing. For instance, New York is the gateway of the Union. There we see illustrated, among other things, in ways that are unique, the problems that arise from the vast immigration into this country. Columbia College has established a chair of sociology, in part to study the problem in the large, but also in part to read and translate to the people of the United States the book which the city of New York spreads out before our eyes. Similarly, Chicago is the great railroad centre of the United States. If I were shaping the destinies of the University of Chicago, I should strive night and day to acquaint the people of the United States with the terms of that problem, in the confident hope that some day there should come forth from the University of Chicago a man who would be of immense service to the country in connection with this question. Here in Baltimore you are face to face, as no other city university in the United States is or is likely to be, with the race problem. If we are not to look to the Johns Hopkins University for light and guidance upon that problem, to what university in the country shall we look? If we cannot look to the universities of the country for light upon these great problems, are not the universities of the country failing to perform their part in enabling the people of the United States to deal intelligently with the great questions of our day?

In other words, I plead for a recognition on the part of the university of the importance of current life. I would not detract by a syllable from the value to the country of research in science, or in history, or in political economy, in medicine, in law, in theology, in literature, or in anything else, but I do believe that if the American universities wish to enjoy the opportunity permanently to carry on such researches as these, they must illustrate to the people at all times the value of such researches by making them tributary to the advancement of the best civilization of the day. I do not mean to imply that the university must itself apply the law which the university discovers. That is the business, if you please, of the statesman, the inventor and the practical man. But the university must set itself to discover the truth if it can, and to publish it, upon the great questions of current importance in the life of the country and of mankind, not less earnestly, not less intelligently, and not less thoroughly, than it applies itself to the study of questions of other sorts. Therefore I believe, again, in a city university because it is in the midst of the activities of city life. The tendencies of our times are to crowd the population into cities more and more. The mere crowding of people together creates problems that become more and more difficult to handle, by reason of their magnitude; but the ingathering of people in the cities, if it makes problems, also develops the forces with which to handle the problems.

The strongest men in every department of life turn to the cities, in our day, as naturally as the river flows to the ocean. There is no exception to this law, in my judgment, in the domain of education. Special circumstances may keep special men in small places; but the law is, I have no doubt, that the city universities can command their pick of the men who are to teach, with an increasing certainty as compared with institutions not located in the city. If a university is made great by its men, this advantage which pertains to the city university would be decisive in our day. There is no solitude like that of a crowd, and it is certain that the man who is determined to have it can enjoy as great opportunity for reflection in the city as in the country. The average man may not find it in the city, but the university is not made great by average men. La Grange and La Place carried on their immortal investigations into the problems of celestial mechanics in Paris during the Reign of Terror and the troublous years that immediately preceded and followed it. On the other hand, the atmosphere of the city is vital with energy, so that a man in any department of life is kept constantly at his best by contact with his fellows. The influences that proceed out from a city are felt far and wide. Cities are the natural reservoirs of power, as the mountain chains are the natural water-sheds of a country. A university located in a city, therefore, occupies the position from which its influence can proceed farthest and with the least resistance. The fame of it is carried on the four winds as a part of the reputation of the city itself.

It seems to me a happy practice, this habit of yours in Baltimore, to identify Washington's Birthday with a consideration of some of the large interests that concern a university. It reminds us Americans of the interest that Washington himself took in the foundation of a national university that should be worthy of the American name. It is inspiring to realize how clearly the fathers of the Republic appreciated, not only the familiar truth that the foundations of a free state must be imbedded deep in popular intelligence, but also the other truth, equally indisputable, but far less familiar, that popular intelligence cannot be maintained at a high level by any system of schools, public or private, which is not continually supplied with new power and fresh inspiration from those ancient springs of learning and investigation, the universities. It is well understood, as I have said, not only that the university is different in type in different countries, but also that within the same country it has been marked by different characteristics at different periods. Nevertheless, whatever may be its type in any country, or whatever may have been its predominant characteristics at any time, the university has always and everywhere been a school for the perpetuation of the accumulated knowledge of the race and for development of its highest scholarship according to the conceptions of the time. The singular thing is, that the men who founded this Republic in the midst of conditions so new, and where everything was so completely undeveloped, should have discerned with such unfailing sagacity the importance to the country of the development here of institutions of the highest learning.

Every decade since the formation of the government has added to the importance of cities in their relation to the destinies of the Republic. I count those Americans happy, therefore, who, during their students days at the university, become familiar with the atmosphere and life of a city. They are likely always to be able to serve their country better in later life, because they know something about one of these busy centres of human industry and activity. And I count it a circumstance for profound and patriotic gratitude that, in these closing years of the century, great universities are being developed here and there in our American cities, within which to train the natural leaders of the best and most disinterested thought of the times. Happy is the democracy whose broad door of opportunity opens to its humblest member, through the public school and the university, an undisputed right of way to the highest eminence of human knowledge and the widest domains of human thought.

THE ENCOURAGEMENT OF HIGHER EDUCATION

AN ADDRESS

BY

HERBERT B. ADAMS, Ph. D.

Professor of History in the Johns Hopkins University

DELIVERED ON COMMEMORATION DAY OF THE JOHNS HOPKINS
UNIVERSITY, FEBRUARY 22, 1889.[1] REPRINTED, MARCH, 1898

I.

The choice of the twenty-second of February for the
Founder's Day of the Johns Hopkins University will always
be recognized as singularly appropriate.   Historic associations, at once local and national, determined the choice.

A local institution, with a national character, was planted

---

[1] This address, first published in the University Circulars, March,
1889, was the first public appeal for State aid to the University,
and is here republished because its general spirit is in accord
with similar appeals more recently made on Commemoration
days. The historic argument, by comparison, is even stronger
to-day than it was ten years ago. St. George L. Sioussat, a Maryland student, has, in foot-notes, revised some of the more important statistical statements and brought them up to date. Compare also Mr. Sioussat's supplement to President Adams' address
on "State Aid to Education," p. 15. To oppose the principle
of State aid to a non-sectarian university is to oppose the whole
current of American educational history and the enlightened spirit
of Thomas Jefferson, who convinced Virginians more than seventy
years ago that a State should develop its intellectual as well as
its physical resources. What constitutes the true glory of a State,
coal mines and tobacco, or statesmen like Washington and Jefferson? Is genius found oftenest in high places or among sons
of the people?

in Baltimore by our President and Board of Trustees in the
centennial year of the American Republic.   Assembled
here under the very shadow of Washington's monument, at
a time when the whole country is preparing to celebrate the
inauguration of the first and of the twenty-third President
of these United States, we cannot but rejoice that the first
President of our Baltimore university was inaugurated on
the birthday of the Father of our Country.

On this national holiday, when the general government
is approaching its hundredth year, on this happy anniversary when our fair *Academia* is just entering her teens,—

> "How tall among her sisters, and how fair;
> How grave beyond her youth, yet debonair
> As dawn,"[1]

it is fitting that loyal Hopkinsians should recognize their
double debt of gratitude, on the one hand, to our generous
local founder; and, on the other, to George Washington,
Father of the National Idea in University Education.

It is a fact not generally known that the Father of his
Country, before he became President of the United States,
was the president of a Virginia college.   Indeed, Washington would never have had a fair chance in public life if, as a
young man of seventeen, he had not passed a satisfactory
examination in surveying before the faculty of William and
Mary College.   Here, for merit, he was appointed to his
first civic office as a county surveyor.   This office gave him
a thorough acquaintance with the western frontier of Virginia, and prepared the way for his subsequent successes in
military and civil life.   When Washington was chosen to
the office of chancellor of William and Mary College, suc-
ceeding the Bishop of London in that educational honor,
he assured the Board of Trustees of his firm confidence " in
their strenuous efforts for placing the system of education
on such a basis as will render it the most beneficial to the
State and the republic of letters, as well as to the more ex-

---

[1] From Sidney Lanier's Ode to the Johns Hopkins University,
read by the author in Hopkins Hall, February 23, 1880.

tensive interests of humanity and religion." Washington was always the friend of William and Mary College, his *alma mater*. Without forgetting local institutions in Virginia, he advanced during his eight years' presidency of the United States to what may be called the National Idea in University Education. From that idea Baltimore to-day can derive encouragement and inspiration.

Washington's grand thought of a National University, based upon individual endowment, may be found in many of his writings, but the clearest and strongest statement occurs in his last will and testament. There he employed the following significant language: " It has been my ardent wish to see a plan devised on a liberal scale, which would have a tendency to spread systematic ideas through all parts of this rising empire, thereby to do away local attachments and State prejudices, as far as the nature of things would, or indeed ought to admit, from our national councils. Looking anxiously forward to the accomplishment of so desirable an object as this is, in my estimation, my mind has not been able to contemplate any plan more likely to effect the measure than the establishment of a *University* in a central part of the United States, to which the youth of fortune and talents from all parts thereof may be sent for the completion of their education, in all branches of polite literature, in arts and sciences, in acquiring knowledge in the principles of politics and good government, and, as a matter of infinite importance in my judgment, by associating with each other and forming friendships in juvenile years, be enabled to free themselves in a proper degree from those local prejudices and habitual jealousies which have just been mentioned, and which, when carried to excess, are never-failing sources of disquietude to the public mind, and pregnant of mischievous consequences to this country. Under these impressions, so fully dilated, I give and bequeath, in perpetuity, the fifty shares which I hold in the Potomac Company, . . . towards the endowment of a university, to be established within the limits of the District of

Columbia, under the auspices of the general government, if that government should incline to extend a fostering hand towards it."

Here was the individual foundation of a National University. Here was the first suggestion of that noble line of public policy subsequently adopted in 1846 by our general government in relation to the Smithsonian Institution. The will of James Smithson, of England, made in 1826, was " to found at Washington, under the name of the Smithsonian Institution, an establishment for the increase and diffusion of knowledge among men." A simpler educational bequest, with such far-reaching results, was never before made. Whether James Smithson was influenced to this foundation by the example of Washington is a curious problem. Smithson's original bequest, amounting to something over $500,000, was accepted by Congress for the purpose designated, and was placed in the treasury of the United States, where by good administration and small additional legacies (in two cases from other individuals) the sum has increased to over $700,000. Besides this, the Smithsonian Institution now has a library equal in value to the original endowment, and acquired by the simple process of government exchanges; and it owns buildings equal in value to more than half the original endowment. During the past year, as shown by the Secretary's report, the institution was " charged by Congress with the care and disbursement of sundry appropriations,"[1] amounting to $220,000. The National Museum is under the direction of the Secretary of the Smithsonian, and the government appropriations to that museum, since its foundation, aggregate nearly two million dollars. The existence and ever-increasing prosperity of the Smithsonian Institution are standing proofs that private foundations *may* receive the fostering care of government without injurious results. Independent administration of scientific institutions may coexist with

[1] Report of Samuel P. Langley, Secretary of the Smithsonian Institution, 1887-88, p. 7.

State aid.   It is a remarkable testimony to the wisdom of George Washington's original idea, that Andrew D. White, who, when president of Cornell University, happily combined private endowments and government land-grants, lately suggested in *The Forum*[1] the thought of a National University upon individual foundations.   This thought is a century old, but it remains to this day the grandest thought in American educational history.

George Washington, like James Smithson, placed a private bequest, so that the general government might extend to it "a fostering hand;" but in those early days Congress had no conception of the duties of government towards education and science, although attention was repeatedly called to these subjects by enlightened executives like Thomas Jefferson, "Father of the University of Virginia," James Madison, James Monroe and John Quincy Adams. It took Congress ten years to establish the Smithsonian Institution after the bequest had been accepted and the money received.   Unfortunately George Washington's Potomac stock never paid but one dividend, and there was no pressure in those days towards educational appropriations from the United States treasury.   The affairs of the Potomac Company were finally merged in the Chesapeake and Ohio Canal, which became a profitable enterprise, and endures to this day.   What became of George Washington's "consolidated stock" of that period, history does not record.   Jared Sparks, Washington's biographer, thought the stock was "held in trust" by the new company for the destined university.   There is probably little danger that it will ever be thrown upon the market in a solid block by the treasury of the United States, to which the stock legally belongs, unless the present surplus should suddenly vanish in armored ships and coast defences, and the general government be forced to realize upon its assets for the expenses of the administration.

[1] *The Forum*, February, 1889.

George Washington's educational schemes were by no means visionary. His stock in the James River Company, which, like the Potomac Company, he had helped to organize, actually became productive and was by him presented to Liberty Hall Academy, now Washington and Lee University, at Lexington, Virginia, where General Lee died and was buried, having served his native State, as did George Washington, in the capacity of a college president. Washington raised Liberty Hall Academy to what he called "a seminary of learning upon an enlarged plan, but not coming up to the full idea of University." He meant to make it one of the three Virginia supporters of the University at Washington. Liberty Hall, or Washington College, his own William and Mary, and Hampden-Sidney, were all to be State pillars of a national temple of learning.

Washington's dream of a great University, rising grandly upon the Maryland bank of the Potomac, remained a dream for three-quarters of a century. But there is nothing more real or persistent than the dreams of great men, whether statesmen like Baron von Stein, or poets like Dante and Petrarch, or prophets like Savonarola, or thinkers like St. Thomas Aquinas, the Fathers of the Church and of Greek philosophy. States are overthrown; literatures are lost; temples are destroyed; systems of thought are shattered to pieces like the statues of Pheidias; but somehow truth and beauty, art and architecture, forms of poetry, ideals of liberty and government, of sound learning and of the education of youth, these immortal dreams are revived from age to age and take concrete shape before the very eyes of successive generations.

The idea of university education in the arts and sciences is as old as the schools of Greek philosophy. The idea was perpetuated at Alexandria, Rome and Athens under the emperors. It endured at Constantinople and Ravenna. It was revived at Bologna, Paris, Prague, Heidelberg, Oxford and Cambridge under varying auspices, whether of city, church or state; and was sustained by the munificence of merchants, princes, prelates, kings and queens. Ideas of higher education were transmitted to a new world by Englishmen who believed in an educated ministry and who would not suffer learning to perish in the wilderness. The collegiate foundations laid by John Harvard in Massachusetts and Commissary Blair in Virginia were the historic models for many similar institutions, north and south. George Washington, the chancellor of William and Mary, when he became president of a federal republic, caught up, in the capital of a westward moving empire, the old university idea and gave it national scope. There upon the Potomac he proposed to found a National University, drawing its economic life from the great artery of commerce which connects the Atlantic seaboard and the Great West. As early as 1770 Washington described this Potomac route as "the channel of the extensive and valuable trade of a rising empire."

Was it not in some measure an historic, although an unconscious, fulfilment of that old dream of Washington when, a hundred years later, Johns Hopkins determined to establish upon the Maryland side of the Potomac a university with an economic tributary in the Baltimore and Ohio Railroad, which follows the very windings of that ancient channel of commerce? Forms of endowment may change, but university ideas endure. They are the common historic inheritance of every enlightened age and of every liberal mind; but their large fulfilment requires a breadth of foundation and a range of vision reaching beyond mere locality. Universities that deserve the name have always been something more than local or provincial institutions. Since the days when Roman youth frequented the schools of Grecian philosophy, since the time when ultramontanes and cismontanes congregated at Bologna, since students organized by nations at Paris, Prague, and Heidelberg, since Northern Scots fought Southern Englishmen at Oxford, university-life has been something even more than national. It has been international and cosmopolitan.

Though always locally established and locally maintained, universities are beacon lights among the nations, commanding wide horizons of sea and shore, catching all the winds that blow and all the sun that shines, attracting, like the great light-house of Ptolemy Philadelphus on the Island of Pharos, sailors from distant lands to Alexandrine havens, or speeding the outward voyager.

Doubtless Johns Hopkins, like George Washington, had no very definite conception concerning the world-wide relations of a great modern university; but he saw as clearly as did the Father of his Country that the beneficent influence of higher education, if properly endowed, must reach far beyond the limits of a single State. His bump of locality was larger than that of most founders. He made special provision that a part of the benefits of his institution should be extended over at least three great American Commonwealths—Maryland, Virginia and North Carolina, from which States his first wealth as a merchant had been drawn. But Johns Hopkins was a railroad-king as well as a merchant-prince. He had economic interests, far and wide, upon land and sea. His wealth came from western as well as southern connections. It came with every train from the coal regions of Western Maryland and Virginia, with every cargo of wheat and corn from the grain belts beyond the Ohio. Johns Hopkins knew well that a great university, like a great railroad, must have its distant feeders, its through routes, and outward connections, as well as its local accommodations and way stations. What a joy it would have been to that man of large enterprise and of broad views to hear that the University which bears his name is to-day honored and respected in every European country, in India, China and Japan; that our university publications and scientific exchanges belt the globe; that Baltimore offers opportunities for advanced instruction which attract students not only from the home-States of Maryland, Virginia and North Carolina, but from every section of these happily Reunited States. Practical business man that he was, *he* would have recognized with the quick instinct of a far-seeing mind and with the shrewd sagacity of a student of railroad reports, the significance of the following statistics, patiently gathered by a student[1] who abandoned even a government office in the treasury department of the United States for the sake of studying at the Johns Hopkins University.

The Baltimore public has been accustomed to see or hear some new thing every year with regard to the number of students from this city, from Maryland, Japan, and each individual State of the American Union. The following facts represent a novel grouping of students according to the great sections of country from which they come. There have been some misapprehensions in our community concerning the region benefited by this university. Our new arrangement of statistics shows that during the present year there have been studying at this institution 98 graduates from the South, 47 from the West, 26 from the Middle States, 18 from New England. It is plain that this university is drawing college men from the same sources as those from which John Hopkins drew his wealth, namely, from the South and West. In the undergraduate department there are now 139 students from the South, 18 from the West, 14 from the Middle States, and 4 from New England. Plainly, most of "our boys" come from the same sections of country as our graduates. The sum total of men from the South is 237; from the West, 65; from the Middle States, 40; from New England, 22. In short the South has more than three and one-half times as many representatives as the West, six times as many as the Middle States, and more than ten times the number from New England. The total number from all the other States combined is nearly doubled by the South.[2] About one-half of

[1] W. B. Shaw, subsequently connected with the State Library at Albany and compiler of the bulletins showing from year to year a comparative summary of State legislation.

[2] For the current year, 1898, the numbers are: from the South 370, from the West 91, from the Middle States 52, from New

our entire student public comes from the State of Maryland.
Considerably more than one-half comes from the three
Southern States which Johns Hopkins wished especially to
benefit. From this brief review of statistical facts, four
points are clear: First, the intent of our founder has been
realized; Second, the South and the West are chief sources
of our student-supply; Third, in these directions are the
lines of least resistance and greatest influence for the Johns
Hopkins University; Fourth, one-half of our student public
comes from other States than Maryland, a fact indicating
that the local idea is happily balanced by the national idea.

There are pleasing evidences of internationality in the
life and influence of the Johns Hopkins University. Some
of our professors came hither from England and Germany,
as did the professors whom Thomas Jefferson introduced
into the University of Virginia. Almost all the members
of our faculty have studied at one time or another in
European institutions. The annual register for 1888 shows
twelve students from Canada, seven from Japan, and one
representative from each of the following countries: China,
England, Germany, Mexico, Italy and Russia. Here is a
New Year's greeting to the president of the university from
four of our Japanese graduates now holding educational
posts in their native country: " Mr. Sato being in town
[i. e., Tokio, the capital of the Japanese Empire], we four
Johns Hopkins University men had a dinner together, and
talked over the good times we had in Baltimore. We
thought we would send greetings to you and remind you
that in this distant East there are some who remember
J. H. U. with gratitude and affection, and who wish every
success to the university. Signed, Kuhara, Mitsukuri, Sato
and Motora." Mitsukuri is professor of biology in the

England 42. This year the South has over four times as many
representatives as the West. over seven times as many as the
Middle States, and about nine times the number from New England. The number of students from the South is, as it was ten
years ago, double the number of students from all the other
States.

University of Tokio, and Sato is acting president of his
alma mater, the Imperial College at Sapporo, and at the
same time he is confidential secretary of the governor of the
Province of Hokkaido.   From the local government board
of that province there came this very year two officials to
study American local institutions at the Johns Hopkins
University.   This mission was at the instance of Dr. Sato,
who, when he was in Baltimore, wrote a doctor's thesis
upon the " History of the Land Question in the United
States," [1] a monograph which, in the opinion of a scholarly
Senator in Washington, contains the best existing account
of the famous Ordinance of 1787 for the government of
the old Northwest Territory.   Since Webster's famous de-
bate with Hayne of South Carolina, that Ordinance has
been the subject of historic dispute.   When Japanese contribute to the enlightenment of American statesmen, upon
American history, let us not begrudge foreigners a share
in Baltimore academic training.   They pay for the privilege
in honest work or good money, and set all American students a good example in not asking something for nothing.

What becomes of our native born when they graduate
from the Johns Hopkins?   Have they as good a record as
the Japanese?   As far as heard from, none of our American
graduates have become college presidents;[2] but, like the
great American people, we have a good deal of presidential
material constantly on hand, and can supply demands on
short notice.   When Clark University, up there on the
Massachusetts and New Hampshire frontier, wanted an
administrative head, the Johns Hopkins promptly sent one
of its best professors for the important office.   That professor, when he set out upon his missionary undertaking,

---

[1] Johns Hopkins University Studies, vol. IV, Nos. 7-8-9.
[2] Since 1889 four Hopkins men have become college presidents:
John H. Finley, now President of Knox College, Galesburg,
Illinois; Albion W. Small, sometime President of Colby University,
Waterville, Maine, and now Professor of Sociology in the Univer-
sity of Chicago; C. H. Chapman, President of the University of
Oregon, Eugene, Oregon; and G. W. Smith, President of Colgate
University, Hamilton, N. Y.

like Augustine when he set out to convert the Anglo-Saxons, selected a little band of men from his own cloister, —devoted men, who were willing to take their lives in their hands and go far hence among those fierce college-tribes of New England.

The blood of martyrs is the seed of the Church. In the interests of science and the higher education, the Johns Hopkins University is ready at any time to throw its best men to the lions—to those young lions, the colleges and universities that are roaring with hunger in every State amphitheatre. Changing this bloody metaphor to a more humane and pleasing form, we might liken the attitude of this university towards all academic suitors, to that of a benignant father of a large family of girls in one of those over-populated, feminine towns of Massachusetts, towards a courageous young man who asked the privilege of marrying one of the numerous daughters: " Take her, my son! take her! God bless you! *Do you know who wants another?* " This is a true story, taken not from town records, but from family tradition in a Puritan household, where nobody is supposed to have ever smiled except at weddings and on Thanksgiving Day.

Seriously, sympathetic friends, such is the conscious self-sacrifice of the Johns Hopkins University. Our dear *alma mater* is willing to give away her sons (and daughters, if she had them) at any time for their own best good and for the good of the country. When, therefore, you read in the newspapers that *another* Johns Hopkins " professor " has been called away (it may be noted that Hopkins graduates are sometimes styled " professors " even before they receive a call), you should greet the announcement with joy and not with grief. Baltimore might as well weep over the latest " engagement " in society circles as to pity the Hopkins for losing her men. What are we here for if not to train up men of learning, science and letters; to establish an academic exchange, a university clearing-house? What better policy could there be than to graduate professors as college-presidents, and students as professors?

Now let us consider a few facts illustrating the fate of some of our Hopkins graduates. The librarian of the historical department, aided by our excellent statistician, has prepared an object lesson for the encouragement of friends of higher education in Baltimore. Upon the centennial map of the United States he has fastened lines of white tape, extending from our Baltimore university-centre in five directions, north, south, southwest, west, and northwest. He has boxed the educational compass. Upon those white lines you will see stars; and they are of various magnitudes. There is a double star over the neighboring cities of Baltimore and Washington, like Castor and Pollux, the great twin brethren, the *gemini* in the American University zodiac,—

> " So like they were, no mortal
>   Might one from other know;
>   White as snow their armor was,
>   Their steeds were white as snow.

> * * * * * * * * * *

> " Safe comes the ship to haven,
>   Through billows and through gales,
>   If once the great Twin Brethren
>   Sit shining on the sails."

From this brilliant *stella duplex*, this double beacon-light, whose rays shine over land and sea, a long belt of pure white light reaches upward to the New England polar star. Clark University is at present snowed under, just below the lowest ray of the great white planet which represents Hopkins academic influence in the remote North. The star is numbered 12. That means there are twelve Hopkins missionaries going up and down in snow shoes, preaching their academic gospel in those foreign parts. Four are now settled on Massachusetts Bay, in such important posts as Harvard University and the Institute of Technology. Two are teaching history and economics at Providence Plantations, where Roger Williams took refuge from his Massachusetts brethren in former days. Four more are at Middletown, Connecticut; and others are down in Maine. New

England once colonized the South with school-teachers from those over-populated towns. Baltimore is now sending a few pious monks, with St. Stanislaus Hall, to return the compliment. In going northward some of our men, four in number, got off at way stations in New Jersey. Thirteen penetrated as far as New York.

Returning to Baltimore, we observe 43 men waiting about the corner of Little Ross and Howard Streets for college presidencies, university professorships, positions in the cabinet or in the United States treasury. Going over to Washington, we note that ten Hopkins men have already established themselves as teachers or clerks in the government service. Pushing southward, we see a white line of Hopkins colonial influence extending from Maryland to Florida. Southwestward and northwestward from Baltimore extend other lines of university colonists, stopping at Austin, Texas, and at Portland, Oregon, where a solitary Hopkinsian is shining like a lone star. Along the white belt the numbered stars represent the number of Hopkins professors and professional men in the various States. Our graduates are particularly numerous in the Northwest. The White Star line westward is a through route from Baltimore and Washington to the Pacific coast. It follows, in general, that old Potomac route, the line of the National Road and of the Baltimore and Ohio, the westward-moving centre of population and the Central and Union Pacific. It crosses the continent to the University of California, where we have three men.[1] By this route our Japanese friends return to their own country and pass beyond our stellar horizon. By this route Hopkins men, like Professors Royce and Levermore, who went out from Baltimore to the University of California, were called back, the first to Harvard, the second to the Massachusetts Institute of Technology. By this route a college lad came from Boulder, Colorado, to the Johns Hopkins University, where he was fitted for a classical

---

[1] Now there are four at the University of California, and thirteen at the Leland Stanford Jr. University

professorship, first in Smith College for women in Massachusetts, then in Bowdoin College for men in Maine. Such are the promenades of Hopkins graduates along these great avenues of travel from east to west and west to east.

The effect of this system of university-exchange upon the country at large is beyond estimate. We see westerners called eastward to college positions; northerners called southwards; and southerners called northwards. A North Carolinian, trained at the University of Virginia, and afterwards at the Johns Hopkins, is appointed professor of history and politics in a Connecticut university, after teaching the same subjects to young ladies at Bryn Mawr. We see a graduate of a Massachusetts college, who took his doctor's degree in Baltimore, lecturing in various colleges throughout the west and finally settling at Vanderbilt University, in Tennessee, whence he makes a weekly trip to lecture in St. Louis. We see a graduate of Harvard University becoming one of our fellows in Greek, then travelling in Europe upon a Harvard fellowship, returning to Cambridge as an instructor, then called to be a professor of Greek in Bowdoin College, thence called to the University of Virginia, to a chair once occupied by our own Professor Gildersleeve. We see our first Doctor of Philosophy in the historical department lecturing at Michigan, Cornell, and Johns Hopkins Universities, all in one year, then holding the chair of economics in two institutions at once, one east and one west, with a half year in each. We see him now in full charge of a department at the University of Michigan and at the same time directing the statistical work of a bureau of forty clerks for the Interstate Commerce Commission at Washington. These are simply representative facts. They might be paralleled by dozens of examples in the history of our various departments of instruction.

What do these facts mean? They mean that the President and Trustees of the Johns Hopkins University have established here a national university upon local and individual foundations. They have realized the historic idea of

George Washington, whose birthday they wisely chose for
their Founder's Day. They have carried out Johns Hopkins' will in a spirit of large philanthropy, transcending the
boundaries of a single State and yet conserving the home
interests of Baltimore and of the State of Maryland.
Whether consciously or unconsciously, they have also realized, in every essential detail, the ideal purposes set forth
in Washington's last will and testament: *They have devised
a plan upon a liberal scale, which has a tendency to spread
systematic ideas through all parts of this rising empire.
They have established a university in this central part of the
United States whither young men are coming from all parts
of the country to complete their education in all branches of
polite literature, in the arts and sciences, in the principles of
politics and good government. By friendship and associations
formed here in Baltimore, these young men are learning to
free themselves from local prejudices and sectional jealousy.*
These phrases from Washington are no longer mere ex-
pressions of hope; they are the language of history.

The Johns Hopkins University has by no means accomplished its mission. Its record is full of accomplished facts,
but facts are only stepping stones to higher things. "*What
you do,*" Hopkinsians, "*still betters what is done.*" All history is but the striving of man towards a better future. Our
academic course thus far has been a constant struggle with
difficulties and a steady advance along the line. We are
entering now upon the grandest campaign in our university
career. It is not a struggle for existence, like that carried
on by Thomas Jefferson for fifty years in the interest of
university education in Virginia, until at last, at the age of
four score, that grand old champion of liberty and learning
won the confidence of democracy, and established an institution which has withstood the shocks of war and recon-
struction. It is not a forlorn hope, like that led for many
years by Col. Ewell, the president of William and Mary
College, when the faculty and the students had all departed
and he was left alone with the chapel bell and a negro serv-

ant, until at last one fine morning a year ago the legislature
of Virginia awoke from its long indifference and voted an
appropriation of ten thousand dollars,[1] which set the old
college bell to ringing again; and a Johns Hopkins man
promptly went down to Williamsburg and took the chair
of history.

Our struggle is for nobler victories than any hitherto
won. We are to grapple with existing facts and, by good
generalship, turn them into favoring conditions for still
greater success. As George Washington said to the trustees of William and Mary, we believe in the efforts of our
authorities *"for placing this system of education on such a
basis as will render it the most beneficial to the State and the
republic of letters, as well as the more extensive interests of
humanity and religion."*

II.

How can the foundations of a National University, rest-
ing upon individual endowment, be further strengthened?
Simply by extension and more endowments of the same
sort. A great university grows as a great city grows, by
the individual association of property investments along
avenues already opened. Watch the present process of
Baltimore extension beyond its former "boundary," and
you will realize how in time the Johns Hopkins University
may extend beyond its original walls and possibly reach as
far as Clifton[2] with some of its buildings. There are men
who dream of founding towns and universities apart from
existing centres of population and capital; but he is a wise
founder who, like George Peabody, Johns Hopkins, or
Enoch Pratt, recognizes the vantage ground of a noble city,
and plants there institutions which will work together

[1] Since 1888, when William and Mary College was revived, it
has received nearly $200,000 in appropriations from the State
and National governments.

[2] Johns Hopkins' country estate at "Clifton" was sold to the
city of Baltimore in 1897 for $710,000.

through coming ages. The principle holds with reference to individual endowments for the higher education. They always accomplish the most good when they are connected with some central foundation which gives them at once stability, unity and individuality, as in the associated institutions of a large city.

Extension by philanthropy and State aid is the manifest destiny of the Johns Hopkins University. There will perhaps be the individual endowment of a college; perhaps of a university library, bearing the name of the giver, like the Andrew D. White Library at Cornell University; of a laboratory, a museum, or an observatory like those at Harvard or at the University of Virginia. Some day we shall have an art gallery like that at Yale. What is most needed, however, is a central academic building and library to shelter fitly the " Fair Humanities,"—the studies of ancient and modern literature; philosophy and ethics; history, politics and social science.[1] Baltimore, in the course of time, will have as many foundations, bearing individual names, as there are now in the older institutions of the country. Glance through the catalogues of Harvard, Yale, Princeton, or the University of Virginia, and see the great host of private bequests, some large, some small, but all of them carefully guarded and applied to specific objects, such as the increase of the library or the support of scholarships and fellowships. There may be as much individuality in a great university establishment as there is in a street or a city bearing a great man's name, like *Washington* Place or *Baltimore*. Probably the families living in the immediate neighborhood of Washington Monument do not regard the individuality of their own houses as lost to view in the general unity and beauty of this noble square with its towering Campanile, its Peabody Institute, its fountains and bronze statues, its Walters Gallery, and its Mt. Vernon Church.

---

[1] Since this address was delivered McCoy Hall has been erected and now fulfills every purpose above designated.

This is an era of educational endowment upon a generous scale. The most recent published report of Colonel Dawson, the Commissioner of Education, shows that the sum total of noteworthy educational gifts during the year 1886-7 was nearly five million dollars. More than two-thirds of the entire amount were distributed among nine institutions, four of them collegiate, one academic, three professional, and one technical. The institution most highly favored was Harvard University,[1] which received from individual sources nearly a million dollars. From one man came a legacy of $630,000. Our nearer neighbor Haverford College, supported by the Society of Friends, received $700,000 in one bequest. Of the 209 gifts recorded by the Commissioner of Education, 25 represent $50,000 or more; 72 were sums between $5,000 and $49,000; and 112 were sums less than $5,000. The most striking fact in all this record of philanthropy is that such a large proportion of the entire amount, fully two-thirds, was given to higher education. The year 1888 is richer than 1887 in individual bounty to institutions of learning. Nearly ten millions were given by three persons for the encouragement of manual training, etc., but there are rumors of even larger benefactions for university endowment. The collective returns for 1888 are not yet published, but it is certain that the past year will surpass any hitherto recorded in the annals of American education.[2]

Whatever forms modern philanthropy may take, one thing is certain, universities are not likely to be forgotten. At the founding of the new Catholic University in Washington, Bishop Spalding said that a university " is an institution which, better than anything else, symbolizes the aim and tendencies of modern life." Will not broad-minded

---

[1] Even richer gifts have been made in more recent years to the University of Chicago, the University of California, and to Columbia University.

[2] In 1895-6 benefactions to universities and colleges throughout the United States aggregated $8,342,728. Of this sum the University of Chicago received $2,200,000.

people in Baltimore recognize the truth of this statement
and strengthen existing foundations? Senator Hoar, at the
laying of the corner stone of the new Clark University, said,
" The University is the bright consummate flower of democracy." Will not American patriots cultivate endowments made by the generosity of sons of the people? Are
the noble gifts of Johns Hopkins for the advancement of
learning and the relief of suffering likely to be forgotten by
present or future generations? All history testifies to the
gradual up-building of universities by individual benefactions. The development of European and American colleges is one long record of private philanthropy. It is not
possible that this generous and appreciative city of Baltimore, this State of Maryland, will fail to encourage and develop an institution which already in thirteen years has educated 770 of its choicest youth, many of whom are now conspicuous for their good citizenship and active labors in
behalf of this community. This city of Baltimore surely
contains individuals with discernment enough to recognize
accomplished facts and with generosity and wisdom enough
to encourage higher education in Maryland in ways that will
do the most good.[1]

While the Johns Hopkins University undoubtedly has
most to expect from private philanthropy, like that which
has already built up the city, it is not beyond the bounds
of possibility to hope that the State of Maryland may some
day extend to our institution what George Washington
modestly called a " fostering hand." At present this State,
by the exercise of its taxing power, takes from the Johns
Hopkins the sum of nearly $11,000 and from the Johns
Hopkins Hospital the sum of $33,000 a year. From our
original patrimony Baltimore County took a collateral inheritance tax of $36,000. The power to tax is sometimes
called the power to destroy. Surely Maryland would not

[1] The total number of Maryland boys who have received
academic training at the Johns Hopkins University is now nearly
one thousand four hundred.

willingly subvert or impair educational foundations that
were laid for the benefit of her own sons and citizens without reference to creed or nationality. The Baltimore public and the Baltimore press only need to consider fairly the
facts and principles in the case to become, if necessary, the
champions of this University in the State legislature.[1]

The exemption of college property, even the property of
professors, from taxation was well-nigh the universal custom in the English colonies of North America. To this
day, Maryland exempts from taxation all buildings, furni-
ture, equipments and libraries of incorporated educational
or literary institutions, with the land appertaining to them—
in other words, all *unproductive* property actually in use for
educational purposes. This principle of exempting the

[1] From a recent official statement it appears that the Johns
Hopkins University has paid in State and City taxes a total sum
of $242,705.64. In this connection may be noted the purchase
by the University from the State of about $1,000,000 in the pre-
ferred stock of the Baltimore and Ohio Railroad, for which $125
per share was paid to the State. Upon this stock the University
has already lost in unpaid dividends the sum of $120,000, which
has been saved by the State. If this loss should prove permanent,
an annual loss of $60,000 (that would otherwise have been
assessed upon the taxpayers of the State) must be borne by the
University. The high price paid for this stock indicates the
opinion generally held by the authorities of the State and of the
University (long after the embarrassment of the railroad company was well known) that the Act of the State making this
stock a first charge upon the gross revenues of the road was a
valid one. In this faith, the sum of nearly $1,250,000 was received
by the State, and now, by the decision of the U. S. Circuit Court,
the income upon this great sum is suspended and possibly lost
by the University.

The Baltimore *Sun*, March 23, 1898, said: Of course, none of
these facts constitute a legal claim against the State. But we submit they lay the foundation for a strong moral claim. Can the
State afford to profit by the loss of a great and noble institution,
founded for no private profit, but for great and useful public purposes, which it faithfully subserves, and which is equally an honor
and a material advantage to the State? The University to-day is
simply in the unfortunate position in which the State itself would
have been but for the University's trust and confidence in the
State eight years ago.

property of institutions of learning is so thoroughly embedded in the constitutional, statutory and customary law of almost every State in the American Union that such exemption may be recognized, like the principles of Roman Law, as sovereign common sense. But some American States go much farther and exempt the *productive* property of colleges and universities, their savings and investments, the income of which is applied to educational objects. The personal property and real estate belonging to educational institutions are exempt from taxation in each of the following States: Maine, Vermont, Rhode Island, Virginia, Kentucky, Kansas, Louisiana, and Nebraska, and probably in others whose statutory laws permit exemption but whose customs and policy vary.

Exemption from taxation is a manifest duty which the State of Maryland owes to an institution which is now using all the income from its productive capital, as well as its buildings, books, and apparatus, for the higher education of Maryland youth. Indeed, one might go farther and say that the Johns Hopkins is doing for Maryland what most States endeavor to secure by large annual appropriations. This institution is to-day discharging the functions of a State University and is paying for the privilege of providing what is usually regarded as the duty of the State to provide.

The encouragement of higher education by government aid, in one form or another, has been a recognized principle of public policy in every enlightened State, whether ancient or modern. Older than the recognition of popular education as a public duty was the endowment of colleges and universities at public expense for the education of men who were to serve church or state. It is a mistake to think that the foundation of institutions by princes or prelates was a purely private matter. The money or the land always came from the people in one form or another, and the benefit of endowment returned to the people sooner or later. Popular education is the historic outgrowth of the higher educa-

tion in every civilized country, and those countries which
have done most for universities have the best schools for the
people. It is an error to suppose that endowment of the
higher learning is confined to Roman and German emperors, French and English kings. Crowned and un-
crowned Republics have pursued the same public policy.
Indeed, the liberality of government towards art and science
always increases with the progress of liberal ideas, even in
monarchical countries like Germany, where, since the introduction of parliamentary government, appropriations for
university education have greatly increased. The total
cost of maintaining the Prussian universities, as shown by
the reports of our Commissioner of Education, is about two
million dollars a year. Only about nine per cent. of this
enormous outlay is met by tuition fees. The State contributes all the rest in endowments and appropriations. Prus-
sia now gives to her universities more than twice as much
as she did before the Franco-Prussian war, as shown by the
report of our commissioner at the Paris Exposition in 1867.
In that year France gave her faculties of higher instruction
only $765,764. After the overthrow of the second empire,
popular appropriations for higher education greatly increased. The budget for 1888 shows that France now ap-
propriates for college and university faculties $2,330,000 a
year, more than three times the amount granted under
Louis Napoleon. Despotism is never so favorable to the
highest interests of education as is popular government.
Louis XIV and Frederick the Great, according to the authority of Roscher, the political economist, regarded universities, like custom houses, as sources of revenue, for the
maintenance of absolute forms of government. The world
is growing weary of royal munificence when exercised at
the people's expense, with royal grants based upon popular
benevolence and redounding to the glory and profit of the
prince rather than to the folk upholding his throne. Since
the introduction of constitutional government into European States, representatives of the people are taking the

power of educational endowment and subsidy into their own hands and right royally do they discharge their duty. The little Republic of Switzerland, with a population of only three millions, supports four State universities, having altogether more than three hundred instructors. Its cantons, corresponding upon a small scale to our States, expend over $300,000 a year upon the higher education. The Federal Government of Switzerland appropriated, in 1887, $115,000 to the polytechnicum and $56,000 in subsidies to cantonal schools, industrial and agricultural; besides bestowing regularly $10,000 a year for the encouragement of Swiss art. The aggregate revenues of the colleges of Oxford, based upon innumerable historic endowments, public and private, now amount to fully two million dollars a year. The income of the Cambridge College endowments amounts to quite as much. But all this, it may be said, represents the policy of foreign lands. Let us look at home and see what is done in our own American commonwealths.

Maryland began her educational history by paying a tobacco tax for the support of William and Mary College. This colonial generosity to another State has an historic parallel in the appropriation of a township of land by Vermont for the encouragement of Dartmouth College in the State of New Hampshire, and in the corn that was sent from New Haven to the support of young Harvard. In colonial days Maryland had her county schools, some of them classical like King William's School at Annapolis. All were founded by authority of the Colonial Government and supported by aid from the public treasury. The principle of State aid to higher education runs throughout the entire history of both State and Colony.

The development of Maryland colleges began on the Eastern Shore. In the year 1782, representatives of Kent County presented a petition to the legislature, saying that they had a flourishing school at Chestertown, their county seat, and wished to enlarge it into a college. The General Assembly not only authorized the establishment of Washington College, which still exists, but, in consideration of the fact that large sums of money had been subscribed for the institution by public-spirited citizens of the Eastern Shore, resolved that "such exertions for the public good merited the approbation of the legislature and ought to receive public encouragement and assistance." These are the very words of representatives of Maryland more than a century ago. Their deeds were even better than their words. They voted that £1,250 a year should be paid from the public treasury for the support of Washington College. That vote was passed just after the conclusion of a long war with England, when the State and indeed the whole country lay impoverished. Towards raising this government subsidy for higher education, the legislature granted all public receipts from marriage licenses, from liquor licenses, fines for breaking the Sabbath, and all similar fines and licenses that were likely to be constant sources of revenue.

The founding of St. John's College occurred two years later, in 1784. This act by the State of Maryland was also in response to a local demand. It was urged by the citizens of Annapolis that King William's School, although a classical institution, was inadequate to meet the educational demands of the age. It was very properly added that the Western Shore, as well as the Eastern, deserved to have a college; and so St. John's was established as the counterpoise of Washington College. The legislative act is almost identical with that establishing the earlier institution, although the appropriation was larger. The legislature gave St. John's four acres of good land for college grounds and building sites and an annual appropriation of £1,750 current money. This sum, in the words of the original act, was to " be annually and forever hereafter given and granted as a donation by the public to the use of said college on the Western Shore, to be applied by the visitors and governors of the said college for the payment of salaries to the principal, professors and tutors of said college." The establish-

ment was to be absolutely unsectarian. Students of any de-
nomination were to be admitted without religious or civil
tests. Not even compulsory attendance upon college pray-
ers was required; so modern were the legislative fathers of
Maryland.

The next step in the higher educational history of Maryland was the federation of the two colleges into the University of Maryland. The two boards of visitors and two
representatives of each faculty constituted the University
Convocation, presided over at Annapolis on commencement
day by the Governor of the State, who was *ex officio* chancellor of the University. One of the college presidents
acted as vice-chancellor. Thus more than a century ago
Maryland inaugurated a State system of higher education
which, if it had been sustained, would have given unity and
vigor to her academic life. But unfortunately, in 1794, the
legislature yielded to county prejudices and withdrew £500
from the £1,250 annually granted to Washington College
and began to establish a fund, the income of which was distributed among various county academies on both shores of
the Chesapeake. This was the origin of the subsidies still
given in one form or another to secondary institutions in
the State of Maryland. In 1805 the remaining appropriation of £750 belonging to Washington College and the entire £1,750 hitherto granted to St. John's College were
withheld for the avowed purpose of " disseminating learning in the different counties of the State."

For six years there was famine in the land as regards the
support of higher education. At last in 1811 the legislature
resumed appropriations to St. John's College. Realizing
that it had misappropriated to local uses subsidies " granted
annually forever " to St. John's, the legislature endeavored
for many years to compromise by giving a smaller allowance. The Court of Appeals ultimately decided in 1859
that such a readjustment was a breach of contract and that
the College could collect what was due it from the State.
There is perhaps some excuse for the economy of Mary-

land in its treatment of St. John's College, namely "hard times." A State that went through the financial crises of 1837 and 1857 without repudiation deserves great historical credit. St. John's College was suspended during the civil war, but appropriations were renewed in 1866 and have been continued, with slight variations, down to the present day. The amount granted in 1888 was $3,000 for the institution itself and $5,200 for boarding twenty-five students, one from each senatorial district.

The first University of Maryland ceased to exist by the act of 1805, which withheld appropriations from St. John's College; but in the year 1812 a new University of Maryland was instituted by authority of the State, in the City of Baltimore. The proceeds of a State Lottery were granted to the institution, for a library, scientific apparatus, botanical garden, etc. The corporation was to have the full equipment of four faculties, representing the arts, law, medicine and theology. Two faculties of law and medicine still perpetuate the spirit of the founders of the University of Maryland, and are honorable and distinguished promoters of professional education. It cannot be said that they were ever treated with adequate generosity, though they actually received from State Lotteries between $30,000 and $40,000, and were never taxed.

The present generation has not been so generous to the cause of higher education as were the Fathers of the State, but nevertheless, Maryland in her entire history has appropriated something over $650,000 for what may be strictly called college education, not counting $60,000 given to the State Agricultural College, nor $40,000 proceeding from State Lotteries. While this collective bounty is small, it is money given by voluntary taxation and not taken from institutions of learning. Most of the amount was raised in times when the State was poor or heavily in debt, and when public money came with difficulty. Moreover this financial generosity of Maryland establishes the *principle* for which we are contending, namely that this State, like all other

7

enlightened States in the world, has recognized the duty of
support to higher and unsectarian institutions of learning.
She has at different times appropriated $650,000 to colleges
and the University of Maryland from her public treasury.

Let us now inquire what other States in the American
Union have done for higher education, always recognizing
of course great inequality in State population and in the
taxable basis.

Virginia, whose earliest educational foundations Maryland helped to lay by her tobacco-tax, has expended upon
colleges and university over two million dollars, during
her history as a State, not counting the colonial bounty to
William and Mary. Since the war Virginia has given her
University $40,000 a year. Before the war she gave $15,-
000 a year. The original university-establishment cost the
State about $400,000. The people of Virginia are proud
of their University, and it would be suicide for any political
party to cut off the yearly appropriation from the institution founded by Thomas Jefferson. The State of South
Carolina was Jefferson's model for generous appropriations
to the cause of sound learning. She has given two million
and eight hundred thousand dollars to that object. Georgia
has given $938,000 for the same purpose. Louisiana has
given $794,000 from her State treasury for the higher edu-
cation in recent years and, according to the testimony of her
own authorities, has distributed over two millions among
schools, academies and colleges. Texas has spent upon
college education $382,000, and has given for higher educa-
tion two and one-quarter million acres of land. The educational foundations, both academic and popular, in the
Lone Star State, are among the richest in America.[1]

Turning now to the Great West, we find that Michigan
has given over two million dollars to higher education.[2]
She supports a University which is as conspicuous in the
Northwest as the University of Virginia is in the South,

[1] See "Statistics on State Aid."
[2] Now (1898) over three millions.

upon one-twentieth [1] of a mill tax on every dollar of taxable property in the State. That means half a cent on every hundred dollars.[2] This University tax-rate yielded last year $47,272.[3] Would the people of Maryland give one-tenth of a mill tax, or a cent on every hundred dollars of their taxable property, to strengthen this University? One-tenth of a mill tax on the present taxable basis of Maryland, which is $486,000,000,[4] would yield $48,000[5] a year. Wisconsin pays one-eighth of a mill tax for her University, and that yields $74,000 per annum.[6] Wisconsin has given for higher education $1,200,000.[7] Nebraska is even more generous to her State University. She grants three-eighths of a mill tax, yielding about $60,000 a year. The State of California[8] grants one-tenth of a mill tax, which yielded last year over $76,000. Besides this, the University of California has a permanent State endowment of $811,000, yielding an annual income of $52,000, making a total of $128,000 which the State gives annually to its highest institution of learning. Altogether California has expended upon higher education two and one-half million dollars.[9]

It is needless to give further illustrations of State aid to American universities. These statistics have been carefully collected from original documents by one among several students, who are making important contributions to American educational history, to be published by the United States Bureau of Education. The principle of State aid to at least one leading university in each commonwealth is established in every one of the Southern and Western

[1] Raised in 1894 to 1/6 of a mill.
[2] Now 1 2/3 cents.
[3] In 1897 over $150.000.
[4] In 1890, $529.494.777. Now estimated to be over $600,000,000.
[5] This would now equal $60,000.
[6] The annual tax is now 17/40 of a mill on each dollar, yielding annually about $254.000.
[7] Up to 1897 nearly $3,000,000.
[8] For 1898 California has raised her tax to 1/5 of a mill. It is estimated that will add $120,000 to her yearly appropriation.
[9] Up to 1897 about four millions.

States. In New England, Harvard and Yale and other higher institutions of learning appear now to flourish upon individual endowments and private philanthropy; but almost every one of these collegiate institutions, at one time or another, has received State aid. Harvard was really a State institution. She inherited only £800, and 320 books from John Harvard. She was brought up in the arms of her Massachusetts nurse, with the bottle always in her mouth. The towns were taxed in her interest, and every family paid its peck of corn to make, as it were, hoecake for President Dunster and his faculty. Harvard College has had more than half a million dollars from the public treasury of Massachusetts. Yale has had about $200,000 from the State of Connecticut. While undoubtedly the most generous gifts have come to New England colleges from private sources, yet every one of them, in time of emergency, has come boldly before representatives of the people and stated the want. They have always obtained State aid when it was needed. Last year the Massachusetts Institute of Technology became somewhat embarrassed financially, and asked the legislature for $100,000. The institution got $200,000, twice what it asked for, upon conditions that were easy to meet.

Can the State of Maryland and the friends of the Johns Hopkins ignore the abundant testimony in favor of the encouragement of university education, not only by exemption from burdensome taxation, but by positive appropriations? If occasion arises, it will be proper and legitimate for the friends of this institution to go before the people of Maryland and say what is needed. *Private philanthropy will do all it can,*[1] but public interest demands that the State should do its part by throwing off needless taxes and settling for what it has already taken away. Will the State

---

[1] To private philanthropy the University owes: 1. Three halls—McCoy Hall, Levering Hall, and the Women's Fund Memorial Building; 2. Two relief funds—one of $105,000 in 1889, and one in 1897 of $234,000; 3. The endowment of 2 professorships, 4 lectureships, 1 fellowship, 5 scholarships.

be thus obliging?   Of course not, unless public opinion and
the Baltimore delegation to Annapolis become our champions.   How shall we influence public opinion and taxpayers?   Tell the facts and publish them.

There are at the present time, in round numbers, 200
students from Maryland studying at the Johns Hopkins
University.   Supposing all those boys should go to Princeton, or Yale, or Harvard, and stay a year, at their father's
expense?   I suppose that $700 a year would be considered
a very modest allowance at any one of these three institutions.   Multiply $700 by 200, and you have the sum of
$140,000 a year, which Maryland fathers *might* expend
either in New Jersey, Massachusetts, or Connecticut.   The
chances are they would not escape so cheaply.   I suppose
it is an underestimate to say that fully one-half the above
sum is annually saved to Maryland fathers by educating
their boys here in Baltimore at the Johns Hopkins University.[1]

Consider another striking fact.   There are 200 Hopkins
students from other States now living in Baltimore.[2]   It is
a very reasonable estimate to say that these students expend, on the average, $500 a year in this city.   Living is
certainly cheaper here than in many northern colleges, and
vastly cheaper than at German universities.   A Baltimore
father now allows his son, who is a graduate of the Johns
Hopkins University, $1,000 a year in Germany.   Allow
$500 annual expenditure by every student who comes to
the Johns Hopkins from a distance.   Multiply $500 by 200
and you have $100,000 a year brought to our city by these
outsiders.   There are now 57 men upon our university
faculty.[3]   It would not be surprising if most of them spent
most of their salaries in this pleasant town of Baltimore.
The university pays out $100,000 a year to its entire staff
of instructors.   A somewhat careful computation has been

[1] The number of students from Maryland for 1898 is 260.
[2] In 1898 over 300.
[3] The faculty numbers to-day seventy-three.

made, based upon the known extravagance or reputed parsimony of every member of the faculty, and the result has been reached that at least $80,000 of this sum is paid back into Baltimore hands for the current expenses of professorial life. Twenty thousand dollars are paid by the university to our fellows and scholars. It is safe to say that every cent of that money is spent in Baltimore. The university gives more than enough free tuition to balance any present charges upon the fellows and scholars. Besides all this, and counting out expenditures for books and apparatus ordered from a distance, the university pays at least $30,000 a year for current local expenses, for coal and gas, for printing our numerous journals, for wages and office expenses. Add up these various items and you will find that the local expenditure by the university and its various members, plus the $70,000 spent and the $70,000 saved by Baltimore fathers in educating their sons at home, amounts to $370,000 a year. Reflect now for a moment that this institution has been in operation for 13 years. Allowing for fewer students and fewer professors and less general expenditure in earlier years, we should be safe in saying that the Johns Hopkins University has caused no less than its original endowment of three and one-half million to be poured into the lap of Baltimore, if we include the taxes we have paid and the cost of our university buildings, laboratories, &c., a local investment, now valued at nearly a million dollars. All this has served to beautify and improve this city, to give instruction to its youth, pleasure and profit to its citizens, and labor to its workingmen. How many families have been attracted to Baltimore for permanent residence by the possibility of giving their sons a good university education? What does a family of culture and fortune expend yearly in this city? My friends, if you will review the whole matter, pencil in hand, after you return home, you will find the estimate of three and a half million dollars local expenditure already caused, directly or indirectly in Baltimore, by this university, a very modest estimate.

It is a painful duty to suggest any measurement of the worth of a great university to a great city by the standard of dollars and cents. We all know in our hearts that there are moral, educational and scientific values beyond all estimate,—products of character, culture and research that can be neither bought nor sold. But we must sometimes appeal to heads as well as to hearts.

Will any Baltimore tax-payer dispute the economic significance of three and a half million dollars expended in thirteen years in this city? Will Baltimore offer exemption to the Belt for eleven years and tax its own university for ever and ever? Will the City Council offer premiums and exemptions to *foreign* capital for investment here in manufactures or in material industries, and impose a tax upon *home* property used for the education of Maryland youth, upon a business, if you please, which brings at least $400,000 per annum into Baltimore circulation? These are considerations which the tax-payers and representatives of Baltimore would not utterly disregard, if properly presented and clearly understood. The Baltimore delegation would willingly champion the Hopkins cause before the legislature, if public opinion and the city press should take our side. The good will of the counties could be enlisted by the same policy as that pursued by all universities that have sought public aid. A free scholarship to the best candidate from every senatorial district of Maryland as determined by a competitive examination set by university authority, would solve the local problem and thus bring higher education into organic connection with the educational system of the State.

Do you say that all this would lead to meddlesome interference by the politicians? That is what everybody said when a university was founded by the Prussian government in Berlin. That is the stock argument against all State universities. But there stand to-day Berlin and all the German universities firm and untroubled upon State foundations. The whole South and the entire West are full of educational establishments by the State. Some of them, like the Universities of Virginia, Michigan and Wisconsin, are beacon lights of intelligent and non-partisan administration. Have Washington politicians done any harm to the Smithsonian Institution? On the contrary, they have indirectly increased its economic power by appropriations amounting to nearly two million dollars. They allow the Secretary of the Smithsonian to direct the expenditure of $220,000 a year. Congress permits the Smithsonian to be managed by a Board of Regents composed of distinguished college presidents and public men of spotless integrity. Amid all the changes in the Civil Service, no man has ever been displaced for political reasons from either the Smithsonian Institution or the National Museum. These facts are stated upon good authority. Are, then, Washington politicians a superior order of beings? Not as far as reported in the newspapers or in the Congressional Record.

There was once a seven years' famine in Egypt, but there were previously seven years of great plenty throughout all the land and much corn was stored up for food in the cities during Joseph's administration. Baltimore, Maryland, and the Johns Hopkins had a longer period of plenty before the lean kine began to come up out of the Potomac. Let us hope that there is corn enough in the store-houses of Baltimore City, and in the corn-belt beyond the Ohio, to make all the lean-fleshed kine once more fat and well favored. In any case Baltimore, Maryland, and this university are all struggling with the same circumstances. As Benjamin Franklin observed about the time Charles Carroll of Carrollton signed the Declaration of Independence, "Let us all hang together, or we shall all hang separately."

What are the serious thoughts that have been emphasized in this address upon "The Encouragement of Higher Education?"

1. The Johns Hopkins is now a truly National University upon Local and Individual Foundations.

2. This noble institution which benefits Baltimore, Maryland, and the whole country, especially the South and West,
can be strengthened most efficiently by further Local and
Individual Endowments.

3. The examples of history at home as well as abroad
show that States encourage universities by wise exemption
from burdensome taxation and by generous appropriations,
if original endowments and private philanthropy prove inadequate.

4. The development of public opinion, based upon a
knowledge of present facts and upon existing relations of
this university to Baltimore and Maryland, is the best way
to encourage Higher Education *in this city, in this State, and
in this country.*

www.ingramcontent.com/pod-product-compliance
Lightning Source LLC
Chambersburg PA
CBHW030550270326
41927CB00008B/1584